Souled Out!

by

Tania Fiolleau

Souled Out

Souled Out! © 2011 by Tania Fiolleau – 2nd Edition
All rights reserved

ISBN: 978-1-936517-12-1

Cover design: Travis Brown
Flightdeck Media
travis@flightdeckmedia.com

Editing: Ari's Editing House
ari@aribert-editinghouse.com

Tania Fiolleau

I Dedicate This Book To...

My loving Grandma Alma for always being there never giving up her faith in me and countless prayers. Grandma, I love you.

My two sons Tyson and Michael. The light of my days and the apples of my eyes. You are my sons, my world, my life.

The girls of the industry and my love and prayers are with you.

My Lord Jesus Christ for dying on the cross for my sins and my redemption. I give you all of the glory!

Souled Out

God told me you have to walk away...

Tania Fiolleau

A word from a friend....

Sitting in front of a glass of my favorite wine, I was thinking of the first time I met Tania. She walked into my apartment with the assurance of someone who didn't know who or what she was about to face. Dressed in casual clothes, her attitude was anything but casual. Her eyes darted around the living room as if she were trapped somewhere unable to find a way out of an awkward situation. The shyness, the timidity translated into a thin smile and agitated manner. It was apparent this woman did not trust easily and it would take some effort to gain her confidence. She sat in the seat opposite mine and wondered, I'm sure, how I was going to broach the subject that brought us together on that Saturday afternoon. After a few minutes spent in the usual 'getting to know one another' chitchat, I asked her to begin to tell me her story. She was eager to get her point across; she did not want to be judged in any way but she wanted me to listen with an open mind and heart. I assured her that I was not there to judge but to lend an ear and be her friend. From that moment on, there was no stopping her. I could hardly keep up with her. I didn't dare interrupt. She wanted to talk, she wanted to cry, and she did both. She poured her heart out. To me it was obvious; Tania had no one to talk to. She had so much that she needed to get off her chest. She had so-called friends, acquaintances and all the rest of it, to whom she would confide from time to time, yet, I suspected she never let herself go into talking to anyone. It was apparent she could not speak the truths that burdened her heart for she trusted no one. She cried on a few shoulders, but she did not relieve herself of the unspeakable horrors she had suffered at the hands of too many unscrupulous men.

Recalling what she said: "How many people do you know have ever had a normal conversation with a prostitute? I'm sure not many of us have. Talking sense, and helping them realize that life doesn't stop with their next shopping spree or their next appointment or their next fix. These women are people. They are somebody's sister, somebody's friend, somebody's mother, somebody's daughter," I began to wonder how many prostitutes she had helped thus far. How many did she help on the road to recovery? As I suspected there were many, many of them she wanted to help but had not reached yet. I have no idea how many of these finally made it out of the hell we casually refer to as 'prostitution', but *"Taking the devil's hand away and replacing it with a loving and caring arm across their shoulders is the way to an exit from this devil's pen. It would be a ladder to climb out of the pit of despair,"* is what will help these girls out of the industry – one way or another.

Tania is kind – an innate kindness that you can only feel and not describe. With this kindness and a listening ear, Tania is managing to *"show them the way to a better, more constructive life."*

Roxane Christ
April 2010

Souled Out

My BoBos My Life My Son

You never will know how much I love you
It's far more than words explain
I did some things out of desperation
I never meant to cause you pain

I haven't always been the best mother
These words to you I'll share
Son, what I need you to know
Is how much I really care

If I could turn back the clock
There'd be so many things I'd change
Practically your entire life
Is what I'd re-arrange

Your worth far more than diamonds and rubies
Platinum or Gold
You are such a priceless gift
For no amount could be sold

You grew up into such a fine young man
And it wasn't all due to my motherly hand

With a heart bigger than anyone's ever been
To me your so perfect, couldn't commit a sin

No matter what, in my eyes
You could do no wrong
I remember when you were little
We'd sing this song...

"I want to stand with you on a mountain"
"I want to bathe with you in the sea"

I'll never forget those days together
Just you and me

You're the best son a mother could ask for
Each day I love you more and more

You've been the biggest blessing to my life
And one day will be to your wife.

I'll end this saying "I love you"
Never forget it, no matter what you do.

Tania Fiolleau

PART I

A Judge's Concern

1.

"You know, Simon, there are so many things troubling me about Ms. Fiolleau's case," Judge Hendrix said, sipping on his scotch. "Too many threads and not a spool in sight."

"I thought it was quite cut and dry," Simon replied, his brow drawn into a frown.

"Not at all. In fact, I would say that we're dealing with muddied waters since the beginning of this affair."

"But, we've heard the witnesses…"

The judge shook his head. "Yes, and we've read the trial transcript, yet nothing in there drives me to a conclusion."

"How do you mean?"

"Simple. Here is a fairly young woman; she has two children from two unions – one a common law, the other a marriage, then we have the husband behaving like something out of the Little House of Horrors wanting custody of the two boys when he wanted the mother to get an abortion with his son. Why?"

"Because he doesn't want them raised by a prostitute. I thought that was fairly obvious."

"That's what we're supposed to see, Simon. Yet, that's not what lies beneath his application for custody."

"What other reason is there, do you think?"

"I think the man does not care if he gets the children or not – he cares not to have Ms. Fiolleau obtain custody."

"How did you come to that conclusion?"

"Look; when Ms. Fiolleau's grandmother took the stand, she showed us photographs of some of the husband's beatings. Photographs which she took."

"Quite gruesome they were."

"Exactly my point. And did we hear any objections from the husband's lawyer? No, none."

"Why wouldn't they object?"

"Because, Simon, if they did, that would have opened the door to his prior convictions and dragged in the fact that he's a convicted criminal. They could not object to Ms. Fiolleau's lawyer building a case against the husband."

"But how did they expect him to obtain custody of two boys when they knew one way or the other the beatings were going to come to light?"

"Two things. One, they tried to demonstrate the beatings were justified – to some extent even denying they happened, but he was convicted of them. Two, they wanted to show that Ms. Fiolleau had no excuse to becoming a prostitute since the husband was wealthy enough to take care of her and the children."

"That's a tall order; I mean trying to justify or minimize any beating is never a way to present a case..."

"I agree, but you see, Ms. Fiolleau was raised as a Catholic and she didn't choose to be a prostitute. The husband forced her into it."

"How? That's not a profession a husband would force his wife into...?"

"No, Simon. That's not the way it happened. You've read it in the transcript. Ms. Fiolleau was gainfully employed by the Ministry of Transportation and Highways and on her way to becoming a First Mate and even a Captain of one of our ferries. Yet, that meant the man would lose control over her. Besides, you've heard her throughout the trial. She kept repeating that becoming a prostitute was a means to an end, and that, if we were to grant her custody of the boys, she would quit the profession."

"I found that hard to believe, actually," Simon remarked musingly. He looked down at the ice cubes twirling in his drink.

"Not so hard to believe when you consider the choice. For one thing, she knows that if she doesn't quit, as the children grow up they would turn away from her. And that, my dear Simon, is something she can't even contemplate."

"What about this friend of hers – Rebecca – didn't she say that she couldn't believe how the husband treated his wife?"

"Again, that's an important point. She portrayed Ms. Fiolleau as the caring mother. She could not comprehend how a husband would treat a loving mother in such a way. She depicted the husband as a spiteful beast whom she had witnessed abuse Ms. Fiolleau, which in fact was an impression that could have marked points for the plaintiff."

"You got me on that one!" Simon didn't understand. "How?"

"You've got a woman raised as a Catholic, portraying a husband enraged by his wife's behavior. She had to believe something was wrong with the marriage. To her, no man would beat his wife without reason."

"But she showed how abusive he was..."

"Exactly. Yet, there had to be a justification for such a behavior. What did Ms. Fiolleau do to provoke him?"

"Nothing that I could see. The defense did not come up with any way that she could have provoked her husband into beating her."

"Again, that's my point. You see, everyone who's testified on the husband's behalf showed him to be a

Souled Out

caring husband and one that would give his wife everything she wanted – so what could drive a man to such abuse?"

"What about Ms. Fiolleau's mother?"

"What about her?"

"Well, I seem to remember her mentioning how Ms. Fiolleau had been treated as a child. Basically, she lived in a dysfunctional family. Wouldn't that have instilled some rebellion in her behavior?"

"Yes, and it's that fear of seeing her own children beaten or maltreated – which they were – that drove Ms. Fiolleau to behave the way she did. Any sparks of argument, or even an innocent threat or gesture on the part of the husband, would have driven her wild to protect her boys. She became a mama bear that would go to any lengths to protect her cubs."

"But why marrying the guy in the first place, let alone have a child with him, if she was afraid of him and what he would do to his offspring?"

"She had to marry him, Simon!"

"Don't tell me; it was another one of these forced choices?"

"Precisely! You see, and again, Ms. Fiolleau already had one child out of wedlock, she – as a Catholic – didn't want another bastard child. Besides which, she had been partly raised by a grandmother who was a devout Catholic and who would not have approved of another child entering the family without being issued from a consecrated marriage. She had already enforced a marriage when her own daughter became pregnant before being married. She wouldn't have taken another comparable situation lightly. Ms. Fiolleau didn't want to let her grandma Alma down again."

"All right, but that only shows that Ms. Fiolleau is mindful of family ties, it doesn't show her as a good mother."

"That's where my problem resides, Simon. How can I be sure she will be a good mother, if she only shows acceptance and obedience of everyone else's rules?"

"What do you mean?"

"Open your mind, Simon. Here is a woman who's doing everyone's bidding – up to a point – and when she's cornered by circumstances beyond her control, she reacts and all her claws are out. What if the husband she's got today turns on her? What happens then? Is she going to walk out and try to hide behind something else in spite of it all?"

"Only time will tell, I suppose."

The judge shook his head and emptied his glass. "Let's get back to my chamber and review some of the statements, shall we?"

"At this hour?" Simon seemed to have other plans.

"No time like the present, dear boy."

As they entered the building, the guard acknowledged the judge immediately and accompanied him and Simon up the elevator to the top office floor. There were only a couple of law clerks milling about quietly and no one else was disturbing the ominous silence permeating the entire floor.

"Boy, this place is like a tomb," Simon commented as both of them made their way to the judge's chamber.

The judge threw an amused glance in Simon's direction. "And that's the way I like it," he said, opening the door of his office. "Okay, let's sit at the conference table – the files are all there anyway."

The first thing that grabbed Simon's attention was Tania's photographs. "I thought I heard you say that you had enough of seeing these," he remarked, pointing at no less than a dozen photos lined up on top of the table.

"Yes, that's what I said in court, you're right, but I have pulled them out for a different purpose than sullying Ms. Fiolleau's reputation."

"What's that?"

Tania Fiolleau

"They all show a beautiful woman, posing for the camera – not for the men in her life."

"What's the difference?"

"When you go to the museum and look at the nude paintings, what do you feel?"

"Nothing!" Simon was smiling. He now understood what the judge was getting at.

"Exactly my point. If you look at these photographs out of the context of the trial, you're only seeing a gorgeous woman depicted in sexy poses. Nothing in any of these pictures would provoke all that much arousal. It's only when the dirty mind of some of the men in our profession label these 'photos' with words, such as 'prostitute' or 'whore', that we feel a sense of desire."

Souled Out

"But these were posted on the website to get clients..."

"No, Simon, they were not. That's where we went wrong. We believed the plaintiff's lawyers, because that's what they were determined to show us. However, when I read the statements – in particular that of Ms. Fiolleau – I found quite a different explanation. These photos"—the judge passed his pointed index finger along the row of pictures—"were meant to attract people to her website where she wanted to sell calendars along with these photos; another way to make money. Money to fight for custody of her kids."

"Are you saying that she got more than what she bargained for?"

"Yes. Exactly. She had no idea at first that men would want to spend time with her. She was an insecure woman..."

"I wouldn't believe it..."

The judge held up a hand to stop Simon's runaway train. "She probably had an idea that the photos would attract the viewers to her site and that they would make appointments with the girls in her brothels, but I don't think she counted on the ultimate reaction that she ended up getting."

"So, you're saying the website was only an

appointment book, or a marketing tool?"

"Yes, that's exactly what I mean. She said it repeatedly, "It's a business, and I am a business woman." And that's what she is. Her mind is not on sex or sexual display. I believe she would prefer hiding under a rock and die right now than having any more of these pictures exposed to slander."

"Alright, I'll bite. What's next?"

"Ha! I'm glad you ask. This is something that will probably sway my decision in her favor."

"What's that?"

"You were not in court when she testified to this"—the judge opened the transcript at a tagged page— "Have a read," he told Simon, sliding the document across the table to him.

Simon's eyebrows shot up when he read, " *Mike did everything in his power since day one to make me get an abortion. He even threw me down flights of stairs saying "kill the baby!" In which she ended up in the hospital for it as well. The first time I miscarried because I was pregnant with fraternal twins so I lost one. When he found out I had a miscarriage he was so happy but it came as a shock that Michael was still inside me and he lived."*

"But wasn't her husband at the hospital...?"

Souled Out

"Her lawyer asked the same question. Read the answer on the next page...."

Simon did as he was told. *"My best friend Wayne was the one that took me to the hospital when this happened."* He closed the folder, a mixture of embarrassment and ill feeling drawing a mask of compassion over his young face. "And I suppose she didn't want an abortion because she is Catholic."

"Yes, Simon. Everything we've heard, everything we've seen, even everything we've read, points us in one direction – Ms. Fiolleau is a Catholic who's taken the devil for a companion and who's now looking for a way out of this mess."

"What about the first boy's father, what did he have to say about the fact that his ex-girlfriend is a Madam now? Would he want his boy to be raised by such a woman?"

"Another good point. And yes, is the short answer. He's testified that he felt the children were in a suitable environment and he had no issues with her as a mother. He was not only a promiscuous fellow in his day, but he never took responsibility for raising his son —her first child. He knew how much of a beast her husband could be. He had met him when Ms. Fiolleau and he were still together. He has picked her up and drove her to battered women's shelters. Yet, the man didn't lift a finger to help her or his son when the chips were down."

Tyson and Michael with Tania

"But he testified on her behalf didn't he?"

"Absolutely. But the only reason he did so is because he didn't want his son growing up in Ms. Fiolleau ex-husband's company."

"Plus, he must have been afraid of the guy."

"Oh yes! He was. In her first statement"—Judge Hendrix opened another folder—"she said, and I quote, *"Dwayne, who was scared shitless of Mike and fought for custody of Tyson and lost, went as my witness and testified that I was a good mother and that he had picked me up one time after a beating and took me to a battered women's shelter. He was so scared but I'm sure that had tons of weight because Mike bribed him with all sorts of things but even he did the right thing in fear Tyson would go with Mike."* Besides, you saw him in court; he couldn't look at the plaintiff in the eye. I tell you, this Mike fellow is nothing but a brute and a bully."

"But if you feel that way, sir, why do you still hesitate to render a decision?"

"Because, my dear Simon, I am watching what's happening in that household. I am letting time tell me if I am right."

"How do you mean?"

"Remember what I asked you at the club? I asked you what would happen, or what Ms. Fiolleau would do if her current husband, this Russian fellow, would lift a hand against her..."

"Yes..., and if she was going to walk out on the situation again...."

"Precisely. But somehow, I think she's doing the same thing with me. She is biding her time, and waiting for my decision. I bet you a dollar that she's going to walk out – whether the man lifts a hand against her or not – as soon as she knows where she stands."

"What makes you say that? As far as I could tell this new husband is just a huge, loving bear…"

"Again, you're right on the money, Simon, but you've already forgotten two things…"

"What?" Simon sounded aggressively intrigued.

"First, you forgot that Ms. Fiolleau is a business woman. She has no intention to remain in the prostitution industry – and she wants to leave this ungraceful past of hers behind."

"But couldn't she do that with him?"

"No, Simon, she couldn't and, mark my word, she won't."

"What then?"

"She'll take her boys and probably devote her life to make penance for what she did."

"And that was the second thing I forgot, wasn't it?"

"Yes, Simon. She is a Catholic woman who needs to repent. The only absolution she will accept – and I mean "accept" – is the one that could repair the hurt she's caused."

"What hurt are you talking about? As far as I could tell, quite a few guys have hurt her, not the other way round."

"What about "her girls" as she called them? Those

are the people she hurt, Simon. She kept them in a business she abhors, and she knows how much this very same business has hurt her. Do you think for one minute, she wouldn't want to repair the damages?"

"I suppose not, but how is she going to do that?"

"That, my dear Simon, I don't know yet."

2.

This last conversation with Judge Hendrix left Simon more than a little curious about Ms. Fiolleau's past. He decided to take a look at her various statements and have a read of her journals. The first of which dealt with her years at home. He reclined in his chair and began what turned out to be hours of reading.

I couldn't say that my father was a proud man, no. He was harsh, demanding and overbearing. Before he became such a beast, and perhaps because of it, he had been raised by a woman whom I felt, could care less about him or his siblings. Fernande, Fern for short, had married a good man but infidelity became a way of life for her. When the marriage broke down, she up and left her husband, Clement, (my Grandpa) and hooked up with a known pedophile – known as "Uncle Charlie." He was in the papers for molesting young boys, and Grandma

Fern was all too aware of this before she married him. This man had a field day with my grandmother's children. He "loved" kids, but since Hank – my father – and his brothers were growing up, they no longer satisfied the man's yearning for fresh, young skin under his dirty fingers. He wanted new flesh to sodomize and to abuse at leisure. In those days, to gather young, vulnerable children under one's roof was easier. He and Fern signed the paperwork and soon opened their home to foster children. As many as they wanted, and as many as he could abuse, came through their door and remained under the "loving" care of that monster, sometimes for years. Grandma Fern only brought foster boys – not girls – to their home, and she was fully aware of what he was going to do to these young boys. Yet it was a business for her and, in my opinion, all she cared about was her paycheck.

When the situation became untenable for my father, he ran away from the horrors he would witness and the memory of what he had suffered during his younger years. He blamed his mother for it all. "Why did she leave my dad? And why did she take us with her?" were questions that must have roamed his thoughts incessantly. What Hank had endured at the hands of his stepfather marred not only his outlook on life but also, in

Souled Out

my opinion, his respect for women – he had none. He wanted to tame them into obedience. It seemed as though he wanted to impart the rage he felt against his mother onto any woman he met.

He was fifteen when he ran away and began searching for work or something to eat. Of course, he had quit school by then and the only way he could find to earn a living was to become a roustabout in construction sites around the city.

Hank, a European by birth, had an eye for the young women that crossed his path. He didn't mind sprinkling their beautiful bodies with the lure of romance. Gaining respect from a woman was not in the cards for Hank. Still, he managed to curb his domineering attitude long enough to make a lasting impression onto one little girl – my mother.

She was fourteen years old when the two of them met. Eyes sparkling with the beauty of youth, Claudette fell for Hank's bidding smile and enticing – not to say gallant – manners. They played the game of love; they toyed with their budding senses and thrilled their minds with the prospect of marriage. However, my grandmother, Alma, was a woman of good breeding and of solid Catholic rearing, and allowing a union between her adorable Claudette and that flirting youngster was not something *she could ever contemplate. Nevertheless, when Claudette became pregnant, Grandma Alma had no choice – she had to put things right in the eyes of the Church and in those of the community. Besides, she had relatives in the convent – nuns they were. What would people say if her own daughter was to give birth out of wedlock – unthinkable! And so, months into her pregnancy, Claudette and Hank went down the aisle. She was a mere sixteen when Claudette gave birth to my sister, Tina.*

Hank was a construction worker – a good one by all accounts – as long as he stayed away from the booze. Through hard work and determination, Hank and Claudette found themselves renting a hobby farm that was on the outskirts of town.

As far as I can recall, the house was a small ranch-style two-bedroom affair. The gray wood-sidings were punctuated of single-pane windows. In the winter, my father would spread heavy plastic sheets across each of them to prevent the cold from invading the house. Since we only had a wood-burning stove to heat up the place, we needed all the help we could get to keep the winter outdoors. Since the property spread over two-and-half acres of land, my father had enough space to build a barn to shelter the horses and a chicken coop for the

Souled Out

Bantom chickens that he raised. However, since the forest at the back of the property had invaded the land before my parents moved in, my father had to do a lot of clearing before he could build anything on that piece of property.

The inside of the house could have been welcoming and even charming; the hardwood floors and the simple décor offered many opportunities for any housewife to make it a pleasant place to live. Yet, my mother never took the time to make from this little house a home. My father built several pieces of furniture, like our beds, the kitchen table and the coffee table, but when it came to adorn the house with a few flowers, pictures or anything that would make it welcoming, it didn't happen.

Life seemed to smile upon the young couple until my father took to drinking in excess, and continued smoking pot to his heart content, and eventually developed a cocaine habit.

Contrary to what one would think should happen under such circumstances; my mother never touched an ounce of drug. Although, she developed a strong liking for wine and consuming a bottle or two to drown her sorrow was a common occurrence in our house.

My mother was only nineteen when I made my appearance into their world. I was his little "Tanza Bear," as my father would call me – although I was a graceful child, with long, silky hair and, I was told, the face of a little angel. He had wanted a boy. "I wish you had given me a son," he reproached my mother for as long as I remember.

Quickly, I felt the lack of love, the lack of appreciation in the eyes of my father and in those of my mother. My father would not even come inside the hospital when it was time for me to being born. Instead, he just dropped my mother off at the front door.

I could not do anything about it all but retreat into my thoughts, my dreams or run to the barn and climb onto my horse. Silver was not a horse of any notable breeding or even handsome, but to me he was the most beautiful horse that could ever be. He would understand my pain, and let me sleep on his back; my arms wrapped around his neck and cry tears on his fur. I found comfort in his company and found solace in the caring for the farm animals. I would go down to the rabbits' cage, crawl into it, put one of them in my lap, and cajole it and kiss and cuddle it. The animals gave me the love that I wanted so badly from my parents.

I sought love everywhere. I would gather flowers from the field and bring them to the neighbor with one goal in mind, that of receiving gracious recognition for the

Souled Out

gesture. As a little girl, I remember going next door and cleaning my neighbor's fireplace as often as I was allowed in her house, for I so liked the appreciation I got for doing so. I would draw pictures of the woman's house or the garden and bring my sketches to her – not to my mother, or my father. Subconsciously, I probably knew they were a lost cause already and that they would not give me any recognition anyway.

I dreaded weekends most. My father was home then, and with his rowdy friends he would drink, get into his stash, and drive my sister and me into retreat. Since I was always in contact with Grandma Alma – a woman I adored – during many of these intolerable weekends, I would take refuge in her embrace. She had food in the pantry, which she laid on the table every time I would come round. She was a portly woman and one that knew how to take care of a family and of a child my age. Any time things got too unbearable at home; I would take off and go to my grandmother's house. Her house was picture-perfect inside and out. It was a two-storey building with two bedrooms downstairs and two upstairs. Built in the late sixties, it afforded all the modern amenities of the time, especially a well-provisioned fridge that my cousins and I would always raid. There were always chocolate bars in there and countless goodies in some cupboards or other.

One of the things that provided me with hours of delight, were my grandmother's wigs and high-heel shoes. She had them on display over Styrofoam heads on the shelves of her bedroom. I would usually take one of them, dress-up, and wear her high heels to prance about the house, imagining that I was perhaps a princess, or a wealthy lady. Besides playing dress-up, I would paint the Styrofoam heads with make-up and design faces on each of them to Grandma Alma's utter dismay.

When my cousins were visiting, we would gather all of the pop bottles we could find either in the basement, which wasn't finished, by the way, or in the trash and pack them in a large bag. We would carry the bag to some place where we would get money for the bottles then go to the second-hand store where we could fill up a bag as much as we wanted with treasures all for a dollar. My business instinct was already in high gear even at that young age. We brought so much junk back to Grandma's place – now that I think about it; I could easily have become a hoarder out of habit.

Souled Out

Talking about things being unbearable at home; could you imagine a house with dirt everywhere – grime and muck thick on the windowsills and mildew where ever it could gather. I remember one day scraping the window ledge with a knife – just trying to get the mildew, grime and filth off my bedroom's window sill. I remember thick amounts of dust on the TV and the furniture. I remember the house being infested with fleas and literally seeing them jumping all over me. Besides not cleaning, my mother didn't seem to care if we had three square meals a day, or even one for that matter. The cupboards were empty more often than not. I repeatedly went back to the same cupboard hoping food would magically appear in it. When I called her attention to it, being hungry, she blurted some excuse or other or told me that she had to wait for dad to give her money to go shopping. Yet, I knew there were other reasons for the lack of food in the house. Money went to buying booze or drugs for my father. I remember my father used to wake up in the morning and sit on the toilet talking on the phone for hours. One time, he came out of the bathroom and when I went to use the toilet, I found a sandwich bag full of cocaine on the floor. When I gave it to him, he simply stated that it belonged to his friends. I knew exactly who it was for. Admittedly, we were poor, but my father was earning enough of a living that we could have had food on the table every single day.

The dogs we had would roam free around the house, too. Although they were very well trained, they would defecate in our room because my mother was often too lazy or ignorant to open the front door for them. My sister and I would let the revolting things dry and then shove it under each other's bed – making a game of it. All the while, my mother seemed completely oblivious to the situation. She wouldn't move from the couch. She would sit on it all day, watching soap operas or just simply stare into space. Even when I called her attention to the dust on the furniture, she would shrug. As little as I was, I knew this was a disgrace. My instincts told me – taught me – to be clean. Perhaps my grandmother's blood flowed through my veins in more ways than one. Over the years, I tried to understand my mother's apathy. In her depressed state, my mother would sit for hours on end looking dazed or absent. To this day, she tells me that my father has changed but in my opinion, he is worse in so many ways. The reason I say that he's worse is because he still plays the blame game. To me it's just evil for it shows that he has no conscience. She says that it was just the way my father was and that she, or others, couldn't do anything about it. "What was she to do back in those days," she says. Being brought up in a strict Catholic environment, she was married and she had to stay that way "until death do them part." What I didn't understand, though, was that she had a biblical excuse to leave the marriage. My father was unfaithful and he was abusing me. He was abusing all of us! That was all there was to it. Although Grandma Alma had told her to come "home" and leave my father, as many times as she thought her daughter would accept her offer, my mother wouldn't budge. As for my sister, she appeared too weak, helpless and on her own planet to do anything. She seemed to live in a fantasy world and still does to this day – she wanted to ignore what was happening around her. She always had fairy tales going on in her head, which she would convince herself to be true and would try to convince others as well. For my part, I was aching from unrelenting emotional and physical pain. It was too much for me to bear. Anytime I would go to my father to spend time with him, most often, he would tell me to "hit the road." One time he told me this in the driveway, so I literally walked up to the road in front of the house and I "hit the road." I was angered and cried until I turned around – perhaps I was hoping he would chase after me, but he didn't. I came back and told him that I "hit the road" just like he told me to, and again, he told me to "go away."

The social services had been alerted of the things that were going on at home and when my sister was an early teenager, they took her away. She went to live with an uncle first but my father took his violent rage out on that uncle for accepting to take Tina away from him. After that, she went off to live in Alberta. Perhaps, it didn't turn out as well as one would have hoped, but she was well away from my father's grip and my mother's indifference – and for that I was grateful.

However, after her departure, nothing changed. My father continued to beat my mother whenever he was high on drugs or his drunken state would gear his evil behavior. He gave her black eyes, broken arms, knocked her teeth right out – whatever else he inflicted upon her while under the influence. I didn't escape his rage either – it continued and it became insufferable to the point that I went crying into my grandmother's arms as often as I could escape that awful house. It was so bad that one day, Grandma Alma came round with her car and tried to take my mother and me away. Yet, it wasn't to be. My father got out of his pick-up, (he had a gun rack on the rear window) armed of his shotgun, chased Grandma Alma's car with us in it, and ordered my mother and me

Souled Out

to go back into the house while he went on chasing my grandmother down the road.

Nevertheless, I wasn't going to give in to that brute. In the weeks that followed, one afternoon, after spending a weekend at Grandma's house, I went to the social services office, sat down in one of the chairs until someone noticed me, and came to talk to me. I explained as best I could what was going on at home and pleaded with the woman to do something about it. She promised she would. Her name was Connie Traylor.

When my father was told that the social worker was going to pay a visit again and that there would be an internal investigation, he grunted and growled. He got very angry and blamed me for this renewed intrusion. I used to be so scared when my father had to meet with the social workers. The only thing that seemed to offend him most was that he had to hide his hashish pipe and somehow cover up his marijuana-grow operation, and that his home was going to be inspected by a stranger whom had more authority than he did. He couldn't control the situation under these circumstances and that bothered him no end. It was not the fact that he was suspected of abusing his wife and child or of making their lives a misery that aggravated him; it was the fact that he had to hide his drugs, his bottle, and appeared to *be a clean-living man. He wanted to be able to live the way he wanted and have no one say anything about it. This angered him.*

I would get very scared of what would happen after one of the social workers' visits – and justly so. In the days that followed that particular visit, my father was to make me pay for meddling and for going to seek assistance from the social services.

3.

An hour or so into his reading, Judge Hendrix came into the law library, a folder clasped under one arm, and found Simon deep in thought.

"So, she grabbed your attention, didn't she?" the Judge whispered in Simon's ear.

Shaken out of his reveries suddenly, Simon sat up with a jolt. "Oh, what...? Oh, I'm sorry..., I've just been reading Ms. Fiolleau's journal – the early years...."

The judge nodded, deposited the folder on the table and sat opposite Simon. "They're quite telling, aren't they?"

"Yes, sir, you could say that. That mother of hers was certainly not an example any girl could follow."

"Did you read anything about the father yet?"

"Just that he was somewhat of an alcoholic...."

Souled Out

"Yes," Judge Hendrix interrupted, "but did you read what he did to her and her dog yet?"

"No, I don't think I got to that part.... Not in this diary anyway." Simon pointed to the small note book in his lap.

"Here, have a read of this"—the judge handed Simon a sheaf of paper that he had extracted from his folder—"I had these stories copied for review. Her past, as you call it, is frothed of nightmarish games..."

"Games?" Simon's eyes grew wide.

"Yes, Simon, these were all sadistic games played by the male gender of our human race. And these *games* are perpetuated by the more malevolent men of our species to this day."

"Are you saying it is men's fault...?" Simon asked, baffled.

The judge nodded and cracked a smile. "Not really. But I am saying that we have this 'male' trait in our character that is often too domineering for our own good."

"Surely, you don't mean that we're all beasts and that we'll beat a woman if we don't get what we want when we want it?"

"It's all in the balance of one's character, Simon, and no, we are not *beasts*, but we are certainly attracted to the opposite sex, and it takes us a good measure of restraint when face with the prospect of taking a woman to our beds."

Simon looked down to his lap. He was not a man given to such inclinations, but he wanted to hear the judge's take on that point. He lifted his gaze to him. "I suppose some of us have more strength of character than others – I hope so anyway."

"Yes, some of us do. But if I were to ask anyone, which of the known addictions he found most repulsive, his answer would probably be, "drug addiction." He would perhaps reflect the opinion of the majority. However, if we look at the afflictions that we can observe every day, many would turn us to revulsion. Diseases, such as cancer, muscular dystrophy, influenza, aids, hepatitis and the rest of them, metamorphose the body into something we have a hard time understanding. Most of us are lucky to be on the outside looking in. Nevertheless, some of us suffer from a much more devastating disease than those I just mentioned. This affliction does not transform the body, but it kills the soul. It is something that we cannot beat with medication, or surgery, or even cure. Only three percent of the "patients" diagnosed will escape the everlasting torment on their lives. Ninety-seven percent will die at the hands of evil thoughts, heartbreak, emptiness and despair. Yet, many women have deliberately contracted this disease and many were forced into it. Either way it is not a disease that a woman would want ... a walk down the sex trade lane."

Simon shook his head. "Do you really believe that anyone forces all of these women to take their clothes off and have sex with men they have never met before and will probably never see again?"

"Yes and no. Some women are forced into prostitution through human trafficking and pimps, others through circumstances, customs, or their station in life impel them to take the plunge into the deep, bottomless pit of prostitution.

*Unrelenting sadness
at the bottomless pit of prostitution*

"Most women and girls in this profession start out with trying to hide their sadness by purchasing everything they have ever wanted. When they buy something new it's a temporary fix to take the sadness away. They hide behind a mask of beauty and a fabricated smile. They avert their eyes from anyone wanting to take a closer look at them. The shame that soon takes hold of their behavior is like a security blanket. It serves as justification for what they are doing. That until the day they can't take it anymore. Then, they go down the road of temptation once again and they try smoking a joint or snort some cocaine on occasion, or they even get into a heroin or crystal meth habit. When they go down that path, the next port of call is the street. However, many of these women start out on the street, being pimped or they start out in a brothel being human trafficked. One thing leading to another, they soon enter a vicious cycle that calls for them to sell their body for money, money for their pimps or traffickers, money they will use for buying drugs and drugs that will keep them right where they are – in the street – until they die from being murdered, committing suicide or from an overdose.

"Without a shadow of a doubt, in my opinion, men could be despicable beasts. However, to put all men in the same bag would be unfair and unjustified. Nevertheless, those who seek sex outside of their relationships are only animals responding to the vilest of instincts. They have absolutely no respect or concern for the women who entertain them. They return to the brothels or pick up a girl at the corner of a street for only one reason: to get a fix for their sexual addiction. Even if they are "happy" in their marriage or relationship, they need more. They need a "different" partner and they need it *now*. When their crisis is over, they offer the excuse that their partner is no longer interested in having sex with them. However, it's often the other way round. They are not interested in having more of the same with that partner who's devoted her life to them, in many cases but not all.

"Prostitutes are not the only ones suffering from the shame perpetuated by their actions – many of their "Johns" are as well. Most of these men cannot let anyone know that they've bought a woman last night. They can't let the cat out of the bag for fear of losing their reputation if not their life in the process. I have spoken to many men that feel guilty after reaching their climax of intense pleasure and regret it until the next urge comes about. I have also spoken with many that simply are hobbyists and get off on degrading and abusing these women. It's a vicious cycle, it's an addiction that's hard for them to quit."

Simon had been listening to all this in silence. He had no idea the judge was so deeply interested in the damages perpetuated by the sex trade. "But what could we do about it? It's not like we could stop men to be men, now can we?"

"No, Simon, we can't. However, someone could certainly tackle the matter from a different angle. There is a lot that could be done about this plague, in fact. Pointing the finger or passing the buck is not the solution. Judging a prostitute is not the answer. Such as we try, too often in vain, to take people off the street, we could, with much better results, help the women of the industry get out of the rat race."

"I think I better continue reading," Simon said, shaking his head. "Maybe, Ms. Fiolleau will educate me..."

"She will, Simon, I have no doubt of it."

When Judge Hendrix took his leave, Simon returned to Tania's journal. His perspective of the case had changed. He wanted—no—he needed to understand who this woman was. He opened the journal again and found the pages dealing with Tania's dog....

Souled Out

There were also goats and chicken, and my parents raised Doberman-pinchers on the farm. We had a young dog, beautiful and black she was. Her natural instincts wavered between obeying her master and going after a chicken or two. When my father first caught her, he beat her, to no avail, and tied the dead chicken to her neck until it rot and stunk, in hopes that it would stop her from killing anymore. However, the temptation was too great and the chicken too alluring a prey not to try again. That day, my father jammed a cartridge into the barrel of a 22-gauge shotgun and fired. The bullet grazed the poor animal's head. While she bled from her wound, her eyes turned to me to help her. She trusted me. We played together all the time. I was helpless; in shock and in fear of my father and I stood there, paralyzed. All I could do was watch. The next thing I knew, my father took a stone and bludgeoned my dog to death in front of my eyes as she whimpered to me for help. She tried to get away from my father. Her skull was breached open; the skin peeling back and her brains starting to fall out while my father continued to bludgeon her until life was smashed out of her. The memory is as vivid as it all happened yesterday. The images are still crystal clear in my mind. I was sad, scared and felt helpless as she looked up at me for help while my father killed her and I couldn't do anything for her. I felt I let her down because she trusted me. She looked up at me to protect her and I couldn't. It still haunts me to this day.

When it was all over, I stood up and shouted, "I hate you!" at his face and ran into the house and into my room face down in my bed and cried hard. For me to speak out in such words to my father was something I have never done before. I feared him too much. My fears were true for he chased after me in a fit of rage and when he advanced toward me he growled, "You hate me? Did you say you hate me, huh?" and a wooden spatula in hand he beat me until his fury abated. I had blood-blistered welts all over my body and I was covered with bruises. These welts were huge blisters filled like bubbles of blood. They weren't your average blisters. The wooden spatula was not the ordinary spatula you find in the kitchen drawer. It was a thick, wooden, flat paddle that he had hand crafted especially to beat on us! 1 _ ft long and _ inches thick. He had made a hole at the bottom tip and laced a leather strap through it to hang it on the kitchen wall. He even stained it to make it esthetically pretty. He was quite proud of it actually. He kept it close at hand – so that he could grab it anytime he felt we needed a hiding. When I woke up the next morning, I felt sick but my mother told me to get dressed and to go to

Souled Out

school anyway. She wanted me to go to school not because she cared about my education but because she didn't want the nuisance of having me home. Anytime I asked for her help with my homework, she never helped me. She even gave me a long-sleeve, blue, turtleneck sweater and a pair of pants to hide my blistering welts and bruises, so that no one would be aware that I had been beaten again. However, in the school bathroom, I showed my school friend, Simone, what my dad had done to me. I asked her not to tell the teachers for I was too afraid of what he would do to me. Nonetheless, the teachers were alerted. I remember a social worker showing up at school with some of my belongings in the back seat of her car. It's pretty sad that I still remember the color and design of that sweater to this day.

I remember times my father would make me kneel on the floor for a long time with my hands straight up in the air and I had to look directly at the wall. He would tell me that if I scratched my nose or even moved one finger or toe that I would get hit with his homemade wooden spatula. I remember this very clearly because it's virtually impossible for anyone not to move even a toe for any lengths of time. And he would watch, just hoping and waiting for me to move. My back and knees hurt until I could no longer stand it. He would make me kneel for so long, it was sheer torture; my arms ached from having to hold them high above my head for all that time.

Because I could never keep my mouth shut, if you think that his punishment stopped there, think again. My father knew how much I loved my horse, so the next thing he did was to give Silver away. Not only did I see my dog being killed, but I also saw my horse being taken from me. He gave my horse away! My Silver! He was my solace. Although, he never gave my sister's horse away. What did she do not to deserve the same punishment as I received? More than likely it was because she kept quiet about many things and I didn't.

I only saw cruelty in my father's gaze, when others saw charm. I only saw indifference in my father's manners when others saw his tempting looks. I only saw a deprecating smile on my father's lips when others saw gentle teasing in his grin. He dominated our lives with the glare in his eyes.

One night I woke up in the middle of the night to see my father in a drunken rage on top of my mother, beating on her. He was very drunk and I ran to try to pull him off her, telling him to stop. He backhanded me sending me flying into the diamond-mirrored wall and made me go back to my room. I lay on my bed crying as I listened to my mother get beaten. There was nothing I could do

Souled Out

about it. Another time, my father was lying on the kitchen floor with a gun telling me he was going to shoot himself in the head. I ran to the cupboard where I knew he kept bullets and I hid them. He lay on the floor drunk and crying, threatening to shoot himself right then and there in front of me.

Day after day, I longed, I yearned for the love I so dearly needed within my mother's arms. What I got was ignoring shrugs or resentment. All I ever wanted was my parents' love.

Closing the journal, Simon got up, took his briefcase and coat, and made his way downstairs to the parking lot. He had had enough for tonight. His mind was abuzz with everything he had read thus far and what Judge Hendrix had told him.

As he sat in his car, he felt the sheaf of paper the judge had handed to him earlier that night. Simon wanted to get home before he read these pages. He knew they were going to stir something in him. He had seen prostitutes paraded in the hall of justice as if they were cattle led to the slaughter, and never paid any mind to them. Until that day, Simon was, as many men, indifferent to their plight or even their very existence. For him, these women served a purpose – not a salubrious or even commendable purpose but a purpose nonetheless. For him, they were slaves of their own *chosen* profession. But after he had heard what Judge Hendrix told him that night, he had his doubt this was indeed a *chosen* profession. Were men in fact so base as to ignore what was going on? Were men willfully ignorant of the fact they used other human beings to satisfy a passing desire? He shook his head and continued driving, deep in thought.

When he pulled up into his driveway, he looked up at his house – a house he had chosen with the greatest of care – and wondered if the day would come when he would be bringing home an escort. "Never!" he exclaimed, slamming the car door. The thought appalled him. Yet, he was still a young man and as good-looking as he was, he had the pick of the proverbial litter when it came to choose a woman as his date or even pursue a relationship with one or another.

He took his coat off as he passed the threshold, put the briefcase down by the desk in the den and went to the liquor cabinet. He poured himself a large scotch and went to sit in his favorite chair.

He pulled out the sheaf of paper out of his pocket and began reading again.

Souled Out

...I am one of them. I had to make a choice. It is either that or risk losing my sons to a brute that very easily could kill my eldest son and me in a fit of rage if I can't stop him by getting custody of both my children. Believe me; my eyes were wide-open when I stepped in the first brothel I had ever seen in my life. The devil took me by the hand then and showed me the color of money – lots of it. I could earn four-day's pay in an hour. With that money, I was able to retain the services of a good lawyer, and hopefully get custody of my two sons and protect them from danger. However, and for the majority of women entering the prostitution industry, the lure of wealth goes much further than that. For many of us, wealth equals happiness. "I wish I could win the lottery." I'm sure everyone has pronounced these words at one time or another. I have, on numerous occasions. Providing that you're young, decent looking and have somewhat of a head on your shoulders, you can earn buckets-full of money. But that's when troubles start.

I made the choice to be a prostituted woman because, at the time, I saw no other way to earn big money fast. Although I went to college and I am somewhat educated, I had no time to get out there and earn a large sum of money overnight. Literally, I had until the end of the *week to find $5,000 to retain a lawyer and try saving my boys from a brutal, obscene future. Same as many girls do every day, I went on my first date, and then another and another. I earned $1,700 on my first night out. Back in 1997, that was a great deal of money. Even today, it is.*

When I went home, I could scrub my body as much as I wanted, I could not wash away the filth and dirt that had already surrounded my heart and soul. As the expression goes, "I felt dirty." Nothing could erase the images from my mind. They are carved in my memory forever. The beautiful get-ups, fancy frills of leather and lace is nothing but a cover up to make the money and hide the pain, sorrow and depression that most people do not see; the feelings of emptiness and daily pain. Women like me carry a very heavy burden; people just don't see it. They are slowly dying internally. People see happiness and glamour, which is nothing but a façade for extreme pain and depression.

Sex should be enjoyed by the couple who loves each other. Sex is a moment in time and space, which brings happiness and closeness into the marriage. It is not something to be taken lightly or with disregard for the loving kindness it entails. It is a beautiful gift from God that is not to be taken for granted. Nonetheless, sex is too often taken as an act of release for the tension endured by men during the day. Many men come to these brothels seeking release. They seek entertainment and relaxation or even sweet talks with someone they hardly know, and won't recognize if they cross paths tomorrow. Some "Johns" request to have sex with the same woman over a long period, even years, but all the same, when their occasional but steady partner dies or is nowhere to be found, they ask for someone else as if the person was just a lovely figure they enjoyed, until it was discarded because it had been broken beyond repair.

Surviving the disease demands strength of character. As I said, I made a conscious choice to become a prostitute, but I also knew that I would not do this for years on end. Like most women in that trade, I am tempted to buy everything I can afford and then some. While I was able to retain an attorney and fight for custody of my boys, I was also able to purchase a house, cars, clothes, shoes, jewelry and everything my heart desired, at the detriment of my soul. I am getting unhappier day by day. Although I have reached the top rung of my professional ladder – I am now a madam – I see myself being destroyed physically, emotionally, spiritually and mentally. My spirit is broken, shattered with every passing day. Every time I am with a client, it takes a piece of my soul. Slowly but surely I am going down the hill of despair. On the outside, I appear to "have it all" but on the inside, I have nothing at all.

****

Although it is gang members that are the main financial contributors to my brothel, I always make it a point never to see any of them myself. I have to draw some lines when it comes to whom I see.

One night, a client came in and chose me. He picked the mirrored room. As its name describes, this room was covered with mirrors on the ceiling and on two walls; black lights and leopard prints on the other two walls. My price at the time was $100 for nude massage, $200 for a hand job, $300 for a blow job, $400 for a straight lay and $500 for half and half. He was grinding me on the price and wanted full service but didn't want to spend more than $300. I stuck to my guns and he settled for the blow job but was not happy about it at all.

While performing my sex act, he put his hand on the back of my head and pushed really hard so that I would deep-throat him. He did it in a degrading manner.

I looked up at him and said, "Don't do that!"

Souled Out

"What the f... do I care?" he retorted. "You're just a stupid whore!"

I got up angrily and said, "A whore?"

"Yes! Slut!"

"No!" I yelled to his face. "And it's because of pathetic pieces of shit like you that I am able to pay for my custody case, you f.... goof! Get the fuck out of here!" and I left the room abruptly.

Anyone who has any street smarts would know that "Goof" is a forbidden word in the trade. People get killed for using that word.

I didn't realize it then, but this man was a member of the Hell's Angels' gang.

He came out to the front lounge with his vest on, pointing at his Hells Angels wings logo, yelling, "You f... bitch! Do you know who I am? Do you f... know who I am? I will shut this f... place down!"

I thought he was going to hit me. I told him to do whatever the f... he wanted. I told him that I didn't give a f... and to get out of my brothel.

He thought that being a Hell's Angel and using his gang intimidation would scare me, but I was at a point in my life where nothing worse could have happened. I honestly didn't give a rat's ass anymore. It was bad *enough I had to perform sex acts on these goofs; the last thing I was going to do was to let them treat me this way.*

****

It is common practice for the local police to go on their rounds to various brothels, making sure everything is okay and checking for illegal immigrants or underage girls. The bylaws state that all the doors to the rooms must have a clear glass window for full viewing. The girls and the clients don't like this because then anyone walking down the hallway could see what they are doing inside the room. The girls and I then came up with an idea; I installed red flashing lights in the rooms and I put a coat hanger with a couple of robes just over the glass to hide the people inside from view. However, if the bylaw enforcement officers saw the blocked windows, we would get fined. When you reach your allowable number of infractions there is the possibility of being shut down. The police and by-law enforcement officers always want to catch us off-guard by running up both the front and back stairs very quickly. The bylaws also state that we can't have locks on both the front and back entrances. This makes it so much easier for them to catch us in the act. I have a button right by the front desk, so that as soon as they run up the stairs, a red light flashes in the room and

Souled Out

the girls and clients know to take the robes off the doors and make themselves presentable.

One day this happened. One of my ladies was in a room with a client. They were right in the middle of some vigorous sex – she was on all fours when the police officer came in the room. She knew she was caught and so did he. Yet, they just continued on until they were finished, right in front of the officer, who stood motionless, watching them. He got so turned on by what he saw, that he took the girl aside, got her information and booked an appointment a week later to see her and do the same thing.

When we have the health inspection or the fire department come in, to be honest with you, they don't even inspect anything other than the girls and they just pass us. They, too, are regular house clients.

There are some clients that are very tricky. They tape a small metal prick in between their fingers and poke the condom as they put it on them so that it breaks while they are having sex with the girl in hopes to pass on sexually transmissible diseases – men are viciously insane at times! At other times, when they have a girl on all fours they try to roll the condom off their penis so that it would just roll off inside the girl's vagina. Later, they play dumb about it.

Tania Fiolleau

****

It never surprises me at all that probably 99% of the men that come into my brothel are married with kids. In my opinion most men eventually cheat. It's in their nature. I know that everyone I have been with has. People tend to think that the type of men that frequent brothels are different than what they are when in fact they are doctors, lawyers, priests, firemen, NHL hockey players, famous actors, rap stars, political figures, etc. I know this all too well because I am the one they call when they want to keep their dirty little secrets hush-hush. There was one priest in particular who would come to the brothel every single Sunday after church with his priest clothing and white priest collar on. He wanted the youngest looking girl I had and would ask her to dress up like a little girl and request that as she was having sex with him to say "daddy, daddy don't. I don't like this daddy." Many of the girls would be upset at this and understandably so, because many of them had probably said the same thing to their father when they were younger. It was a sensitive issue for them but the girls would all too often comfort one another in situations like these by saying, "It's a good thing that he came to the brothel every Sunday and did that with an actual girl of age than to live out his fantasy with a little girl." What

Souled Out

enables many of the ladies to perform such debasing sex acts, is the fact that they think they are able to save another child from going through something they did when they were younger.

****

In my brothels, the girls are all offering the same prices for their services. That way it is fair and there are no undercutting prices and it keeps the women on top of their game when it comes to their appearance and being "polished", so to speak. One time, a client came in; I greeted him at the door showing him photographs of the various fantasy theme rooms. Once he decided on which room he wanted, I had the ladies come in the room and greet him one at a time and say hello to later ask him who the lucky lady was. I can't even tell you how many times they pick the least polished or less attractive hostess and say "I'll go with her 'cause she looks cheaper." These men honestly don't care with whom they have sex. However, I assure them that they all charge the same prices. One evening a group of five men walked in late on a Friday evening. These men looked just like they walked out of a GQ magazine modeling shoot. They came up to me and said, "Nina, we want the dirtiest, ugliest, fattest, grossest, stinkiest girl you have tonight." I, of course, responded that we are an upper scale *establishment and they went on to say how they were playing silly games as men who get together sometimes do, and one of their buddies had lost a bet so he had to sleep with the worst girl we had. What is wrong with these guys?*

****

Some men that are into the sickest most demented things, believe it or not, aren't the weirdo-type men but the men whom are in powerful positions. They state that they are so tired of being in control in their everyday life that they want to be controlled while with a girl. Some of them actually come with plastic sheets with just a small square cut out of it; they lie down on the floor and cover themselves with the sheet with the hole exposing their face and pay very large dollars to have a woman defecate on their faces. They call it a "hot lunch." Some want a "golden shower" where they lie down in the bath tub and have a woman urinate on them while spitting on them and calling them the most demeaning names. Some want to be tied up, gagged and even asphyxiated. They want the girl to call them every demeaning name in the book, spit on them, smack them, etc. I remember one time I had a regular that would come and see me and give me $1,000 each time to tie his hands behind his back and kick him in the scrotums as hard as I could until he

Souled Out

would fall on the floor in dire pain. With these kinds of clients it's not even about sex it's about them being degraded. I had one client once that as soon as he would walk in the door he would want me to start screaming, yelling and hitting him, pretending I was his girlfriend that was mad at him stating "I hate you, you asshole!" etc. He wanted me to pretend I was his angry girlfriend and no sex. Just some real weirdoes, I'll tell you.

****

I find it so sad how so many women who work for me have boyfriends that don't work yet. These men know what they do for a living and claim to love these women. I tried many times to tell them that if a man loves you he wouldn't let you do this but they just don't see it. Many of these men have many women on the side, all doing the same thing and the women don't even know about each other. It is very common for these men to knock these women up because it keeps the woman with them while they keep making money. They are PIMPS! Masters in manipulation. There is even a book out there that teaches you how to be a pimp, manipulate and exploit these women.

****

I remember a very high profile lawyer. He was so addicted to coke and was such a sex fiend that he spent *all his money on drugs and women. He couldn't even keep the heat on in his house, yet he would hide $100 bills in all kinds of weird places throughout his place to have the girls crawl around his floor naked on their hands and knees, barking, looking for the money. When they would find it they could keep it. I remember one very famous rapper. One of my girls was the lead-girl in his video. None of the girls wanted to go see him because he was so cheap. He didn't want to pay more than half the going price and this is one of the biggest, richest rappers of all time. I had another famous actor and movie producer who used to get girls from me and he would take the youngest ones and when he became comfortable with me over time he asked me if I could find him a girl as young as 13 and even a virgin if I had one. I became disgusted and told him that I don't find girls in the school yard.*

Simon dropped the pages to the floor. He was angry, ashamed, appalled and disgusted, all rolled into one. He had no charitable thought toward any of these women, and that disgusted him. He had no sense of what a so-called drug addicted woman could feel, and that appalled him. The detachment he had felt to this day toward the prostituted women of this world was the

Souled Out

subject of his shame tonight. Ultimately, Simon was angry because his hands were tied – tied to the principles that had guided and had led him such as a light down the path of his life.

He decided he had enough for tonight. He needed to walk away, to break away from the invasion of thoughts that encumbered his mind that evening. He went to the kitchen and began cooking a storm – pasta, meat sauce, salad, and even whipped up some crepe Suzettes for dessert – all of which designed to let his mind wander amid something else than sex.

4.

Simon woke up with a start. He had been dreaming.... Slowly getting his bearings, he got up and went to sit in the den. He couldn't go back to bed until he had read one of Tania's journal.

The day my dog died marked my life and sent me on a further downward slope of loneliness and despair. I no longer had my dog or my horse to comfort me. I had seen my mother being beaten. I had seen my father flaunt his infidelity and crass love at my mother's face. Being only a little girl at the time my father decided to lay his eyes on two of my aunts and set his filthy paws on them, I could not open my mouth, but my eyes were wide open – my father was cheating on my mother with his sisters-in-law – how base can a man be? When I was 17, I realized that my mother was heart-broken. I found out that one of my aunts – who was also a friend of my mother's – had slept with my father. I didn't think twice about it – I tricked her. I called her, asking if I could come over for a visit. When she answered the door, I beat the crap out of her. I was enraged how she could pretend to be my mom's friend and do that to us.

One of my dad's sisters had a son, nicknamed Buckshot, my cousin. For reasons I won't dwell on right here, Buckshot came to live with us and, I guess, my father finally got his wish: a boy – his nephew – to love and control. Later, I considered Buckshot as my brother – which he wasn't – but in a way he was....

One night I once again felt my father bend over me, while I pretended to be asleep. He was crying. I felt he was drunk, and the way he was acting made me very uncomfortable and made my skin crawl. He was pawing me telling me "Daddy loves you" but it felt very creepy. Especially since I used to dread walking by my father any time for fear that he would smack my tush or rub my chest. He did it in a playful way but even at a young age it just didn't feel innocent to me. I suspect he would have tried to take things further if I hadn't screamed at him one day in front of my mother, "Stop touching my boobs!" He never did it again. I guess there are some kids you could get away with it, and some kids you couldn't, and I was one of them. On the other hand, I think Tina was molested. To this day, she denies it, but I feel in my heart that my father was abusing her sexually.

As if he were an annoying bug hovering over my bed, I waved and pushed him away from me one night when he came in my room. The next thing I knew, he went to my sister's bed.... Did he touch her? I don't know because I turned to the wall not to see, and pulled the blankets over my ears not to hear as this was just too often a reoccurrence. To this day Tina maintains that nothing ever happened, yet, I saw the glimmer of satisfaction in my father's eyes whenever I suspected he had had his way with my sister.

Since my father couldn't get his jollies with his daughters – at least with me he didn't – he decided to have his way with our babysitter, Laurie. Oh yes, he raped a twelve-year-old virgin in our barn. But who would be there to help her or to condemn the man when my father bribed her not to say a word to anyone? She told me he raped her, took her virginity while she begged him to stop. She confirmed this to me two decades later –

but everyone knew it happened – when I contacted her after hearing about it. I tried to pressure her into laying charges but she told me she just couldn't bear to relive the event or seeing my father again.

The poor child was scarred for life by my father – how base can a man be? To assuage his guilt, I guess, and to shut the child up so that she wouldn't tell on him, he bought her a horse! Go figure.

Once again, my mother had turned away from acknowledging that my father was nothing more than a drunk, an adulterer, a child abuser and a rapist to boot – all of it without a word of indignation or admonishment. She stayed with him knowing he raped the girl and even went as far as blaming her for it. How sick, weak and selfish could my mother once again be?

When the social services finally took me out of that hell-hole, I saw my mother shrugging off the fact that she was going to lose yet another daughter. The reproach I held for her inaction, her indifference, and her blatant rejection, has been ever present throughout my life and has not yet abandoned me. My parents don't exist anymore. When people ask me about them, I simply say that they are dead. And I'll tell you why; when I got married the first time, my mother gave me away, since

Souled Out

Dad never came to the wedding – I guess she was glad to get rid of me again. My mother had seen the multiple beatings that my husband had lay on me prior to the wedding and she did not try to talk me out of it. As for the second, and the third time, my parents never attended the weddings. I invited my mother to my second wedding to simply have her say, "Why do I need to come to that one? I went to your last one. It's too far to drive." Yet the very next weekend she drove down to stay at her sister's and get together with her girlfriends that she knew since childhood. My sister never came to any either.

    They had denied me love or even care since birth, so why would they show up at any wedding of mine? It was just a continuation of their ignorance of me. As I tell this story, my father is supposedly very ill. He was diagnosed with prostate cancer. I don't know how long he will be here on this earth, and my sister has pleaded with me in the past to go see him and make things right before he passes away. I told her I would never set eyes on him again. Do I sound unforgiving? Perhaps I do. It's not easy to have an ounce of forgiveness for the man who treated me like "the runt of the litter" my whole life and for the woman who sent me to school covered with welts or denied me love or affection or even a smidgen of acknowledgement that I existed. I do forgive my parents.

How could I expect God to love and forgive me if I don't act Christ-like and love and forgive others? I forgive but tears are not for me to cry now. I know, as a Christian woman I am to forgive, however the devil is our enemy, and I simply have seen my parents as demons – I literally have. However I have forgiven them. "For if you forgive men their trespasses, your heavenly Father will also forgive you." (Mathew 6:14)

Perhaps my opinion would be a little different if they were regretful, had remorse and asked my forgiveness, but they still, to this day, blame me for everything, saying I have serious mental issues and that I am a liar. I have no more crying to do or ruefulness to feel or forgiveness to impart although, I have forgiven them. Forgiveness aside, there is nothing but pity for my parents – they simply don't exist to me anymore.

Soon after my departure, I was made a permanent ward of the courts, which was exceptional if not impossible in those days since corporal punishment was allowed back then – the abuse had to be very bad – and my life opened the doors to one foster home after another. I felt as though I didn't belong anywhere. I remember being in the court room with Connie Traylor – I on one side and my father and mother on the other side. The

Souled Out

judge made it clear that I would not be made a permanent ward of the courts if my mom would just take me, be with me and leave my father all together. He asked my mother what she wanted to do. She clearly stated that she wished to stay with my father and give me up to the system. Words can't express the sense of abandonment I felt that day. I was so hurt and feeling rejected. My social worker wrapped her arm around my shoulders as she walked me out of the courtroom and assured me that everything would be okay. If only that statement were true. She took me out for lunch before bringing me to yet another foster home. This is when it even got worse. Every time I started at a new school, not knowing anyone, being very pretty and the new girl on the block, all the boys liked me while the girls instantly got their backs up. I won't hide the fact that at the time I got into many fights. For a few weeks at a time, I would go to one school, and then to another home, and then to another school. And that's when I began seeking love anywhere a glimmer of its presence would tempt me into obvious yet innocent flirt. But, promiscuous I was not. I was twelve years old then and remembered my grandmother's words. She had taught me to save my virginity for the man I would marry one day. I had made a promise to myself that it would be so. I gradually understood that love would not come knocking until I gave it a chance or demonstrated that I could give as much as I wanted in return.

Once again, Simon closed Tania's journal. He wished he could talk to her. Tell her, "I'm sorry for everything...," but all he could do was to keep his own counsel for now and let Judge Hendrix know how different he had felt that night.

5.

When Judge Hendrix arrived in chambers the next morning, Simon was waiting for him.

"How about breakfast, your honor – my treat," Simon said as the judge deposited his briefcase beside his desk.

Judge Hendrix didn't take his coat off and smiled. "Don't tell me – you've got Ms. Fiolleau on your mind...."

Simon lowered his gaze. "I had only a couple of hours sleep last night, and I really need to talk to you about this case."

"All right then, let's go to Stephan and have something to eat before the next session." He looked down at his watch. "We've got about an hour."

Souled Out

Simon nodded and followed the judge out of his chamber.

When they reached the small café, the place was packed – as usual at that hour of the morning.

"Good morning, Judge," Stephan exclaimed genially as the two men came through the revolving door. "I've got a little table by the window for you..."

"That's just perfect, Stephan. Lead the way...," Judge Hendrix replied as he and Simon followed the proprietor to the table in question.

"Okay, Simon, let's have it," the judge said once they had placed their orders and their coffees was on the table.

Simon shifted in his chair. "Well..., it's hard to say, but I've got this feeling that Ms. Fiolleau has another purpose in mind if she were to get custody of her children."

"Could you clarify that thought for me?"

"When I read another few pages of her journal last night, I noticed that she wants to forgive her parents, but she's not reached the point where she could do it yet. She wrote the words, she even quoted the bible, but there is an undercurrent of resentment throughout her journal. That's what brought me to think, she may want something else besides obtaining custody of her kids."

Their breakfast arrived and once the waitress had departed, scurrying to another table, Judge Hendrix said, "Listen, Simon, I know you have not read the whole file, so I'll just answer your question on the point of forgiveness for now. Yes, Ms. Fiolleau would like to forgive her parents for what they have done to her, but she wants much more than that – she wants to forgive herself."

"Forgive herself?" Simon said a little louder than the circumstances allowed. "What do you mean?" He lowered his tone, "She has nothing to forgive herself for; the men who have abused her..., her father..., these bastards should be the ones going down on their hands and knees..."

The judge put up a hand. "Okay, I hear you." He pulled another sheaf of paper out of his breast pocket. "Have a read of this, and then tell me who she wants to forgive and why."

"Have you got anymore of these"—Simon shook the sheets in front of the judge—"I'm beginning to think that you've got a whole file in your pocket." He was smiling now.

Judge Hendrix chortled and then resumed eating while Simon began reading. Unlike the others these

Souled Out

pages were typewritten. Simon was a bit surprised by the fact, but said nothing.

I remember once talking to one of 'my girls' about the world outside of our industry. She had the mind of a fourteen-year-old in the body of a woman of thirty. She only knew two sides of the world she lived in – the side where she lived with somewhat overprotective parents and the side where she dwelled today. She had barely made it out of grade 10 when a bastard raped her. Ashamed to say anything to her parents, thinking the rape was her fault, as most girls do, she decided to take the high road to the low life of prostitution. She left home the following week and with her savings, which were modest, she managed to hit the city full of dreams. She wanted to be a model. She had the body for it. Seeking employment in that industry without falling into the trap of prostitution is tricky. Having no street sense, she soon found herself gainfully employed in an agency that gave her appointments (as many as she could stand) every night. With the money she made, she reached the top of 'her class' in no time. That's when she arrived at my doorsteps. The reputation of my bawdy house had reached her ears and she wanted to be part of a well-maintained, well-frequented brothel. Yet, her ultimate goal, her dream had not changed – she still wanted to be a model. Although getting older by the hour (literally), her appearance, her demeanor and good looks would probably have offered an open door into some haute couture's houses. However, the day we sat down to have our chat, she felt oppressed, incapable to focus on the future. She was trapped into the present – into the day-to-day life of an escort. She could not erase the images of the past. In order to preserve a modicum of sanity, most of us sink into the present, ignore the future and try to forget the past. It is easier to ignore the future than to forget the past and much easier to live in the present – to live for the moment – and set aside the effect it has upon us. However, for Monique, her immediate past was quickly catching up with her. She played the game we all play: try to remember only the good times. For her it was easier than for most of us. She had had a good childhood. The only thing that marred her teenage years was the raped she endured. Her resolve to "make them pay" for what he did to her was ever-present. She wanted every man to pay for what that young rapist did to her. What she did not realize, perhaps, is that she would be re-living the pain every time a man would share a bed with her. Therefore, the memory of those good times was blurred by her obsession to "make them pay". There was no place for the future in her daily planning. There was no means of getting out in her strategy to attain her goal.

The similarities between our stories struck me when I finally decided to look to the future rather than the past. I had a clear goal. I had dreadful memories mixed with a few good ones – of my grandmother Alma, for example – but most of them were blurring my vision of the future. Yet, I would have to take steps to get out of the business, if I want to leave my sons a legacy worth anything in their lives. One of the memories that were most troublesome to me was the one of my father and how my mother chose him over me. As you read by now, my father was not a man that had earned any form of respect from me. All I had ever wanted from him is to be

Souled Out

loved. I wanted to be the little girl he would have wanted. Yet, to him, I was nothing but the "runt of the litter" whom he wished was a boy and he treated me as such.

These days I try talking to him about forgiveness – a word he seemed never to have used in his entire life. He still doesn't want to say "I'm sorry for whatever I've done to you." He still wants to blame me for the love he did not give me. He can't see past today, past the present, and ignore the past. Atoning for his sins will never be something he will strive to attain. One day, many years ago, I went to my parents for a visit. My father got on the topic of my being a whore. The conversation got heated and I told him that it was his fault that I was. I went on to tell him that if it weren't for him beating me, I would not have been in foster care, which led me to run away, in turn to being raped and tortured, ending in my losing my virginity to that monster. My father had the nerve to tell me, "You weren't raped. You were such a whore that you f... the guy for a free ride!" I became overwhelmed with the worst anger I had ever felt. My fear of my father was no more. I went into a fury resulting in my beating on my father. I saw a fear of me gleaming in his eyes for the first time. He ran away to the phone and called 911. For the first and only time in my life, my mother somewhat stood up for me and said to the police, "he deserved it." That was the one and only time my mother sided with me where my father was concerned.

The burden attached to our past is often too heavy for us to bear. We fight to remain ignorant of the events we experienced; we battle to redress a situation that needs no redressing. We can't change the past, yet we try, in vain, to modify it. I am not saying that we are pre-destined (perhaps we are) to do anything. I'm saying that it's up to us to change the course of our lives. We have the power to do so, if only we had the strength to leave the past alone.

As for Monique, I tried to let her know that life was not stopping at the front door of a brothel. There is no rule or law to say you have to remain in the industry. You may feel as if you are forced to do so because you can't do anything else or because you don't know any better. Wrong! You have a choice. You may think the choice is not yours to make, nevertheless it is. You can wallow in the pain of having to serve a few men every night or you can enjoy the freedom of being able to feed the temptations and go shopping until you drop as they say. Or, you can say, "NO!" and close the door on that life for ever. It is within your power to do so.

There are several ways to go about doing this, but before you close the door, there is another that you should open – the door of your past. You need to confront your past, in order to free yourself from it. Making a clean breast of things is far from easy. You are guilty until proven innocent in this game. Unfortunately, this is a fact. Society today is not as forgiving as one would think or as understanding as some people would have you believe. Within that society, there are people who are part of your past. Whether they were cruel and unforgiving such as my father was, or gentle and decent folks such as Monique's parents were, does not matter. They are members of a society that is basically intolerant and does not understand how much they hurt their own when they judge the way

Souled Out

we live (or better said; the way we survive).

Jesus said, "Judge not, that ye be not judged. For with what judgment ye judge, ye shall be judge: and with what measure ye mete, it shall be measured to you again." (Matthew 7:1-2)

You don't even need to be Christian, to read the same precepts repeated time and again from the many philosophers of our times. Yet, this is an unpleasant fact as I said; you will be judge according to the standards of our society. Already, Monique, before she left her home, knew how her parents would judge her. She was afraid to admit what had happened because she felt guilty, even though she was the victim in this case. We are all victims of circumstances – whether good or bad – but we should not be victims of someone else's understanding of our lives. We are all classified, put into a compartment, based on the measures of our society's framework. It seems that our past frames the box in which society puts us. What I am advocating is for us to break the frame, do away with the old box and replace it by a new one. To break the box, indeed, you need to break the links you have with your past. Most madams that have come out and resumed a life that fit within the guidelines of our society will tell you NOTHING. They will not divulge the names of the people involved. They will not reveal the horrors they have witnessed in their pasts. They have broken the frame and interred all memories of childhood or of their lives in the industry deep into the recesses of their minds. That's the only way to regain the respect you have lost from a society who will never understand you or the profession. A mother may forgive a child for its trespass, but other people will not.

There is a poem that, although not well known, has always given me a fresh insight in our world's tolerance.

Desiderata

Go placidly amid the noise and the haste, and remember what peace there may be in silence.
As far as possible without surrender be on good terms with all persons.
Speak your truth quietly and clearly; and listen to others, even to the dull and the ignorant, they too have their story.
Avoid loud and aggressive persons; they are vexations to the spirit.
If you compare yourself to others, you may become vain and bitter; for always there will be greater and lesser persons than yourself.
Enjoy your achievements as well as your plans.
Keep interested in your own career, however humble; it is a real possession in the changing fortunes of time.
Exercise caution in your business affairs, for the world is full of trickery.
But let not this blind you to what virtue there is; many persons strive for high ideals, and everywhere life is full of heroism.
Be yourself. Especially do not feign affection.
Neither be cynical about love; for in the face of all aridity and disenchantment it is as perennial as the grass.
Take kindly the counsel of the years, gracefully surrendering the things of youth. Nurture strength of spirit to shield you in sudden misfortune.
But do not distress yourself with dark imaginings.

Souled Out

Many fears are born of fatigue and loneliness.

Beyond a wholesome discipline, be gentle with yourself.

You are a child of the universe, no less than the trees and the stars; you have a right to be here.

And whether or not it is clear to you, no doubt the universe is unfolding as it should.

Therefore, be at peace with God, whatever you conceive him to be, and whatever your labors and aspirations in the noisy confusion of life, keep peace in your soul. With all its sham drudgery and broken dreams; it is still a beautiful world.

Be cheerful. Strive to be happy.

Max Ehrmann

Simon folded the document and handed it back to the judge. "May I ask where you got these pages?" He resumed eating.

"You may ask, but I am not going to give you an answer. Let's just say that throughout these lines, I can really see why Ms. Fiolleau wants to get out of the industry. She has a great need for repentance as you've read. All these things are not in the transcripts, nor in the files you've read – they're buried in her journals and in these copies of her diaries." The judge emptied his cup. "Besides, I've done some research of my own and there could be a case made against some of the perpetrators she encountered."

"I guess, I better continue reading whatever you've got in that pocket of yours."

Judge Hendrix smiled and asked Stephan for the bill.

6.

Simon Gilbert was in his thirties, not an ounce of fat on him, and a smile that ladies would kill for. However, what made Simon all the more attractive to many was his compassionate attitude. Being brought up in a family that thought him to be respectful of others; he decided to go to law school with one goal in mind: help those who may need counsel and assistance in their time of troubles. For him, going to church and pay one's tithing was not enough when it came to help those who faced the blindfolded justice. He wanted to open their eyes to the path of freedom. His legal degree not only allowed him to be a defender, an advocate on behalf of the people who had barred themselves from freedom, but also, and now, to learn from one of the most respected Supreme Court judges – Judge Hendrix.

Somehow, Tania Fiolleau was going to be his teacher in the matter of prostitution, human trafficking and abused women. Having made up his mind to learn everything he could about this Madam, for the next few weeks, whenever time permitted, Simon plunged himself

Souled Out

in her life through reading her diaries, journals and statements.

I remember being transferred to yet another school and for once I was actually making some decent friends for this was the high-school that my elementary friends went to. One day I was walking down the hallway with all my books in hand and one of my friends came to me to tell me that there were five girls in the bathroom whom had come here from my previous school to "kick my ass." The next thing I remember; Kelly came at me saying, "You want to fight? Let's go." And she punched me right in the face. There was no way I could let everyone at my new school see my getting my ass kicked or it would be difficult staying in that school. I threw my books down, I grabbed her by her mane and I repeatedly knee-smashed her in the face. I gave her many upper cuts, breaking her nose. One of her friends then jumped in. I got her in a head-lock and repeatedly rammed her head in the locker doors. I remember looking up at one of the other girls – I could tell by now that she was thinking twice about jumping in to hurt me. This was one hell of a fight. The principle and teachers broke it up and we got hauled down to the office. There was a lot of blood covering the hallways and none of it was mine. Kelly was in the bathroom in the principle's office, cleaning herself up while we were waiting for him to appear. I snuck in and I lay a beating on her again. I had so much anger and rage in me at that point – I knew I was already going to be in trouble – I didn't care what would happen next. Nevertheless, that little performance awarded me the respect of all the kids at that school. I was then given the nickname of "Golden Gloves." I was the talk of the school as one not to be messing with. This gave me the confidence I needed when I, later, decided to take martial arts.

During my stint going from one foster home to another, I visited my parents from time to time. I can't clearly remember when it happened, but during one of my visits, I brought my father a hashish pipe for his birthday – how silly is that? Yet, I had purchased the pipe in hope that he would give me the love and recognition I wanted from him. All he gave me in return was an opportunity to peddle marijuana to my friends for him. I accepted to do this, simply to gain his approval. He was growing it at the back of the house by this time. I remember there were often burlap sacks filled with marijuana in the dryer – spinning to dry the leaves – and big soup pots of homemade hash he'd be cooking on the stove.

Souled Out

During another one of these visits, I found my mother, my father and Buckshot ready to leave; they were taking Buckshot to the train station and then going to a barbecue at my uncle's place.

My father simply told me they were going out, and added, "Amuse yourself..., 'cause we're gone!"

I was in shock. They knew I was in foster care. They knew I had taken the bus to come for a visit, and now, they were ready to leave; not even acknowledging that I came all that way to see them. They didn't even care. They didn't even invite me to go with them. I looked at the door for the longest time after they left. I could not come to terms with this sort of abandonment and rejection yet again. I had just come to visit them that weekend and they left me...? How could they do that? They had gone to a barbecue to get drunk at my dad's brother, Emile. When I was little I used to go to my uncle's place with them for a barbecue – yet today I had not been invited.

My mother had blatantly accepted to stay with that demon, in spite of the beatings and the abuse, the infidelity, and she had obviously chosen to let me go in favor of staying with him. She chose him over me again! My mother! Then, if that wasn't enough, when I finally managed to come back for a visit, they left to have fun, partying at my uncle's place without even giving it a thought that I might have wanted to go with them.

So, here I was, 12 years of age; my parents had turned away from me, my father had rejected me outwardly, my mother had chosen him over me and even Buckshot was gone....

I had this horrific sensation that I was going to be alone and never being loved for the rest of my life. It might have been the imaginings of a teenager – but all I could see was that for me there was no future. Being alone wasn't an option. My mother, father, sister, Buckshot and my animals were all gone. I had nothing left but foster parents who only thought of me as a paycheck. My pain was too great to endure alone anymore. I wasn't Cinderella. I wasn't going to be rescued from the ugliness of my relatives by an elusive Prince Charming. The fairy tales were no longer part of the consolation prize – they were long buried with my memories of a lost childhood.

I went to the bathroom, looked in the mirror and didn't like what I saw. This was the reflection of someone no one wanted to see. A girl that was invisible to everyone. The image of a girl no one wanted to know – a young woman no one wanted to love. Amid the tears, I had an idea.

Souled Out

Tania was still a child...

I went to the kitchen where I knew my father kept all sorts of pills – outdated medications mostly. I figured there were enough there to do the deed. I went back to the bathroom and I took some, and then some more, and then some more, swallowing all of them, until I felt a little dizzy and the room swung around me. I wrote a suicide note telling them my pain and why I did it. I lay down on the floor until everything faded away amid a fog – and then nothing.

Tania Fiolleau

I woke up several hours later in hospital. I had tried to kill myself and didn't succeed. But who had been there to prevent me from dying? They had all gone to a party.... When Buckshot and my mother came in, I got my answer. Buckshot had forgotten his bag that he was to bring with him to the train station and they had come back for it. He had come to the bathroom door, seeing that I was nowhere in the house, and found it locked. He then alerted my mother that the bathroom door was locked and that something must be wrong. She went to the side of the house, apparently, and Buckshot climbed up to look through the bathroom window to see me unconscious in front of the toilet. My mother kicked the door in and they rushed me to the hospital. My stomach was pumped and my system flushed out. The doctor said if Buckshot would not have forgotten his bag, I would be dead. I realize now that God had a far greater purpose for me here on earth, but I didn't see it then. My grandmother Alma had a prophet prophesied over me. Her name was Mary Goddard. She said I was going to go through a lot of turmoil in my life. She said I was like a little chipmunk running up and down a tree from side to side. She stated that's how I would go through life, taking the winding road but that God was going to use me in an

Souled Out

all mighty powerful way, to help others. I still have the recording of it.

As this story unfolds, you will see that God has sent many Angels my way. There were times when angels were guarding me and seeing to my well-being, but never as obvious as this was. Waking up again in a world that had ignored me since I was born seemed unfair at the time, but I suppose, my task on earth wasn't complete then – and maybe it isn't complete yet.

My father shrugged when he learned what I had done, and promptly sent me back to my foster home. As for my mother, she cried for awhile, but I don't think it was for me that she shed tears – the shame of having a suicidal child that was a permanent ward of the courts was probably more like it. What would the neighbors say? It was already enough that she had to send me away two years after my sister without having that same daughter trying to kill herself.

I returned to that foster home, feeling devastated, but most of all – I was alone again. Some of the foster homes would put locks on the refrigerators and lock the children in the basements while they spent time with their family. I knew they were just in it for the money. We had wieners while they had steak. We had powdered milk while they had real milk, and so on. I remember this one *foster home only allowed us to use three squares on the toilet paper roll every time we had to go to the washroom. I remember I was only allowed three sanitary napkins for the entire length of my periods. Nevertheless, I was never to go back to the farm or that awful house. As young as I was, I knew there was only one person I would tolerate or even love seeing again, and that was Grandma Alma. She knew what I was going through, I was sure of it.*

In spite of it all when I returned to the foster home, I felt relieved. Perhaps it was because I could go back to school the next day or perhaps I felt someone was watching over me – I don't know – but somehow I knew I had been given a chance at life and I wanted it to work.

However, when they told me that I was to leave that place, change school again and move to yet another neighborhood, something in me snapped. I had enough. It was very hard starting over at a new school at that young age.

I can't remember how old I was, but I was in grade 8 by this time. I saw no point in staying anywhere under the "direction" and "guidance" of a social service that had made sure that I hopped from home to home and from school to school in less time that it would take me to unpack my suitcase. I took matters in my own hands

Souled Out

then. I left in the early morning hours one day, and made my way to the main road. I knew I could hitch a ride to the nearest town and maybe take a bus to where ever the few dollars I had in my pocket would take me.

As I was walking east, I saw many cars pass me and totally ignore my presence until a couple of different cars picked me up, taking me as far as they were going, until I hitched another ride and then another. Then a semi came to a stop ahead of me. I ran to it and from the cabin, the guy told me to "hop on" – and so I did.

He asked me where I was going. I told him "where ever you're going will be fine. I just want to get out of this town."

I guess that's all he needed to hear. We drove for hundreds of miles and, believe it or not, I talked to him about Jesus and told him I was a Christian. He told me that he was too; gaining my trust and making me feel relaxed, until he decided to pull to the side of the road at a truck stop. Perhaps my beauty and innocence turned him on. I knew what was going to happen – but I couldn't bring myself to believe it was going to happen to me. "Oh God, please no!" was all I could say. I screamed – but who was going to hear me? I cried – but who was going to care for my pain? I begged him to stop but he wouldn't. I yelled, and fought against his body invading me – but *what was I but the runt of the litter to fight against him? After exhausting my strength trying to fight him off, I realized it would just be easier to let him have his way with me. At this point I could care less if I lived or died. He invaded my body. He took my virginity that I promised I would save for my future husband. At the time I felt as though any virtues I had were now stripped from me forever. My virginity was something I could never get back. My innocence was gone. I literally allowed myself fall into a subliminal world. I lay there as if I were on another planet. I couldn't believe this was happening to me. Why me? When he was finished, he tied me up and left me in the back of the cabin as he drove for many more miles. Then he pulled over and had his way with me again. He raped me, he sodomized me, he controlled me again and again, and again, for a couple of days that seemed like an eternity. He kept referring to me as "a good little girl" for just laying there while he raped and tortured me. To this day I can't stand the smell of oil and leather or the smell of a mechanic's shop, for it reminds me of that dreadful day. There are even a couple of songs I hear on the radio from time to time that he played in his truck, which, when I hear them, trigger horrible memories to this day. I remember the pain as if it were yesterday.*

Souled Out

He was dirty, older and smelled awful. He had the face of a demon. I will never forget him for as long as I live.

During a moment of respite, I found the scissors I always kept in my purse which I used to cut marijuana leaves. I feigned resignation and asked my abductor to untie me, so I could go and sit up front with him. He agreed readily and probably thought he had bent me into submission by this time. As soon as the opportunity presented itself, I plunged the scissors into his side and hung on. He screamed but his reflexes were not good; he stopped the 18-wheeler on the shoulder of the road, which allowed me to escape unscathed, so to speak. I ran as fast as I could into the wild. It was a very cold, wet night and very, very dark.

I ran out of sight and out of reach as far as I could and hitched another ride. In hours, I found myself in the West Edmonton Mall, a thousand miles from home, begging for a quarter from each passer-by – just enough to get me something to eat. But my absence from the foster home hadn't passed unnoticed. Since I was a ward of the courts, the social services' reputation was on the line. They had to find me and bring me back. The authorities had been alerted to be on the look-out for a runaway girl. The police at the mall soon recognized me and it didn't take long for me to be apprehended, handcuffed and led, under guard, to a plane back to my foster home. They led me off the plane with security guards and handcuffs to prevent me from running away again, as if I were the criminal.

Coming out of that ordeal, with shattered hopes, crushed dreams and lost desire for a white wedding, saving myself for my husband, I decided to do something about these filthy pigs.

I suppose, I was like so many girls at that age – disillusioned. I was even in the newspapers with my photo as being in a so-called gang, the "Whalley Burnouts" after that. I simply started hanging with other kids that seemed to have problems as well, and, in some weird sense, it was better than having nothing or no one to care about me – and they never judged me. I had dreamt of saving myself, my body, my soul for my future husband. I had envisioned the perfect wedding, with all the trimmings.... But since it wasn't to be, I thought I would do well to learn to defend myself against these brutes and find a more positive form of stress relief besides drinking and doing drugs. I had seen them in action since I was old enough to comprehend what was happening, and now I wanted none of it for me. Thanks to Connie Taylor – once again – I was able to take Tae-Kwon-Do/Korean Kick Boxing lessons that I requested to

Souled Out

take. I came on top of my class and was a member of the Lebanese American Tae-Kwon-Do Federation. I even got the courage to enter a couple of tournaments.

7.

Tania Fiolleau was definitely a 'fighter', Simon decided. She had demonstrated that trait of character more than once during the trial. That woman had learned to fight for survival since birth. Being raped must have added to her resolve to get out of a life that had only brought her to the edge of a ravine, out of which she was trying to climb and this last, desperate attempt to get custody of her two sons seemed to be the only thing that separated her from the freedom she so richly deserved.

That night, Simon entered another phase of Tania's life. Unbeknownst to him, what he was about to read was going to be a turning point in Judge Hendrix's decision.

At the issue of the rape, I didn't seem to be able to adjust to the foster home's environment; the badgering, and the indignation of it all weighed heavily on my mind. Still in school and with Connie Taylor's approval, I took on a job at a sawmill located miles away from where I

Tania Fiolleau

lived. I went to school at night until I completed Grade 10. The crappy jobs were all mine – men's work in the hands of a small girl. I was driving the forklift, working the plainer and the green-chain, etc., pretty much operating all of the sawmill machinery. A little girl doing a man's job. I didn't mind, though. I was making good money at an age when most teenagers only made a few bucks as busboys or servers at the local McDonald's and it boosted my self-esteem; being able to keep up to these men and support myself on my own. A whole six dollars an hour of it. Ten hours per day with no coffee-breaks and only a half hour for lunch. Moreover, the owner of the mill knew I worked hard and he knew that I needed the money. He told me I could earn a few more bucks by cleaning houses at the sawmill after work so I did that, too, on my days off. I even got a 50 cents' raise on my next paycheck. The only thing that bothered me was the mill being so far from where I lived, and having to get there by 6:00 am before the buses started running. I would have liked to have my own transport to get to the job site on time and not to depend on anyone driving me. However, that meant obtaining a drivers' license and buying a car. As for living at the foster home, I couldn't handle it anymore. I had lived with people who would lock their foster children in their basements after 6:00pm while they had their family time upstairs, who would put locks on the fridge's door to prevent us from grabbing a glass of milk whenever we wanted one. I had experienced strict living with foster parents who belonged to some religious sects and who didn't allow the kids to stay indoors – whatever the weather conditions – while they were out at church or running errands. I tell you; I had it up to here, with these people.

Connie soon realized that I was becoming desperate and I wanted to move on with my life. Ignoring the consequences that could befall her, if it didn't work out, she took the reins and signed on the dotted line when it came for me to be accepted as an "independent youth," whereby I would move into my own apartment, pay rent, obtain a drivers' license and finally purchase a car.

Since I had no furniture when I first moved into my own place, a cardboard box was my coffee table, a bowl and a cup (all-in-one) served as my dishware and I had a hope-chest that one of the foster dads had made for me. (I still have it today, for the same reason that I don't even have anything that my own dad gave me. I guess they were not all bad, come to think of it.) I bought all my stuff at the 'Dollar Store', yet, none of that mattered; I was proud as punch to be on my own and proud to be earning a living however hard the job was at the time. With "independent living" though, came conditions – of course. Connie told me that she needed to be able to come to my apartment, day or night unannounced, and find nothing like drugs or alcohol. In short, she wanted to be sure I would be on my way to live and earn a decent living. I never dreamed of disappointing her, and I didn't. She was my savior. I guess, in a sense, she was another angel sent my way again. She was the one person who believed in me, who believed in my integrity, my resourcefulness and most of all, she trusted me. Besides Grandma Alma, of course.

The next thing was to buy a car. Connie signed for me to get my drivers' license but when I applied for a loan, the bank turned me down. I had no credit reference and although I had a steady job, the bank manager was reluctant to lend me the money without a co-signer. That's when I went back to Grandma Alma. She and my grandfather had followed my steps since birth and were aware how hard I had been working to attain my goal. They trusted me to make good on the loan for the car, and co-signed for it. By the time I reached my seventeenth birthday, I lived in the first high-rise built in a new suburb and I was driving a beautiful, black Fierro sports' car.

Souled Out

While I was working at the mill, I noticed the "coffee truck" coming to the site twice a day. I got to talking to the driver and got interested in what he had to say. His name was Tom and he told me that he had a route all to himself – the best one in the region – that he had developed a good clientele and that he was earning some $60,000 a year, which, in those days was a very good wage compared to my $6.00 an hour. I liked driving; I liked the freedom to create my own business, to have my own clientele and to work as hard as it would take for me to make better money than what I was making at the mill. It didn't take me long to approach the delivery company and to apply for a job. Yet, it wasn't going to be as easy as I thought. The owner figured this petite, all-female, pretty young woman wasn't going to make the cut when it came to drive a truck and feed hungry men on construction sites around the city. The catering company had sixty employees which were all hard-working lesbians besides me and the owner's daughter. Don't get me wrong, I have no ill feelings towards lesbians, it's just that many of them were the butch kind with strong dominant personalities; they could very easily handle these men on the construction sites. He decided to test me. He hired me to scrub the kitchen walls, to give me the worst jobs he could invent, hoping I would quit in a *matter of days. Pulling commercial ovens away from the wall and scrubbing the grease off the concrete walls behind them is just an example of the types of jobs he gave me. However, he had it all wrong. I am no quitter. I scrubbed, cleaned, washed and worked hard until he finally caved in. He assigned a truck to me and gave me a worthless route – again thinking I would not last long after I would be on the road for a day or two and having all these construction guys to deal with – again, he figured wrong. By the end of the year, I was making $60,000 a year. I had added a zero to the route's initial worth of $6,000 and had hired another young woman to take a second truck on the road to expand my clientele, having her work for me. I gave her my route and took good old Tom's route. Our boss knew that building a route needed guts and tenacity more than seniority did.*

By the time I turned seventeen, I was living in a very spacious apartment, decorated with handsome furniture and made a very decent living. For a short while I was feeling as though I was on top of the world until I met Dwayne.

He was a nice enough guy. Although only 5'4," he seemed tall to me at the time. He was all muscles and quite handsome. I was a small girl myself, so he seemed big to me. He was working as a machinist in town and lived with his mother. One of the things that attracted me about Dwayne was his kind and gentle manners. He was eight years older than I was and appeared to have it together. I guess I didn't see the forest for the tree. He was twenty-five, I was seventeen and we developed a very good relationship until it all went south. He was the guy all the girls wanted. Muscular with eighteen-inch arms and driving a brand new, black T-Bird with t-roof, he was the 'bachelor' par excellence.

One time, Dwayne and I decided to take his T-Bird, drive down Interstate 5 and go to California. We were having a blast, going to Disneyland and Hollywood, cruising the streets of Los Angeles not knowing what would be in store for us. The way the streets are down in L.A., you can be in a ritzy area one minute then take a wrong turn and end up in gang territory the next. And that's exactly what happened. We turned down the wrong street. We had the rooftop down and Canadian plates on a hot new sport's car in an alley, which attracted the attention of the wrong crowd coming toward us. In moments, we were surrounded by at least fifteen scary-looking people. I remember they were dark-looking fellows, menacing types. They started swarming our car, *asking us what we were doing, taunting us with disobliging comments and insulting remarks. I became very afraid, knowing that we would be robbed for sure – we had landed in one of the most insalubrious part of town – somewhere we definitely were not welcome. I could see Dwayne panic and I froze with fear. They were opening the car doors and were taking over our car.*

The next thing I knew, out of the middle of nowhere, a very, very tall white man (he looked seven feet tall to me) appeared and almost glided across the alley as though he were floating on air, surrounded by a bubble of angelic light. He fixed his gaze on these men defiantly. As soon as they saw him, fear took over all of them and they ran away for their lives as fast as their legs could take them. Dwayne and I went looking for him but he disappeared and simply vanished into nowhere. To this day I know he was an angel. Why would all these black gang members run in fear from one white man in black gangland territory? I believe it was the fear of the Lord they sensed and this tall man was an angel that God sent to protect us. Dwayne still doesn't believe in God but even he will admit that was something he will never forget or could explain.

Souled Out

For almost three and a half years, he stayed at my place off and on, all the while living at home. We enjoyed each other's company until I got pregnant, and when he refused to share in the household expenses to take care of his child, or found all sorts of excuses not to assume his responsibility, I began to suspect something was wrong. I was a jealous young girl but with good reasons. He would say, "Why should I live with you and the baby and pay half your rent when my mom lets me live at home for free? My mom cooks and cleans for me and does my laundry." Selfish words they were. By this time, he had changed jobs and was now driving five-ton trucks for a living. I was unsettled about it all. One night, I followed his car to the depot and waited until he parked it, and left in his work truck. As soon as I got into his vehicle and started snooping around, I felt something wasn't right. I was enraged at the thought he was cheating on me. I knew it. I could feel it in my gut. I had developed a spider sense at a very young age. I couldn't stand knowing he was spending his nights away from me and deceiving me with other women. Since I was with child by then, the whole thing was all the more infuriating. I rummaged through the car until I found the tell-tale condoms. I took some out of the packets, poured some hand lotion inside them and blew them into large balloons that I tied to his car's antenna. Then, I took my lipstick and graffitied his car with obscenities until my rage was spent and I went home.

In the past, I was judging street girls to be base and disgusting – an insult to God – but until you walk a mile in their shoes, you wouldn't know…. Every one of them has a story.

When Dwayne came home, he was all-denial and to this day he wouldn't admit to paying low-level street workers for blow-jobs in exchange for a six-pack of beer. His good friend felt bad for me and even confirmed it. The disgust I felt at that moment enraged me more than the infidelity. I took no time to send him packing. I went to his mom's house with the baby in my arms, upset and distraught, only to have his mother get in my face and yell at me to get off her property while Dwayne stood beside her. I became so upset; I kicked him in the scrotums as hard as I could (the baby still in my arms). He hit the floor and ended up having to go to the hospital. I guess that Tae-Kwon-Do paid off after all. His mother, later, called the cops and had me arrested and put a peace bond on me. Her son never did anything wrong.

Souled Out

During the pregnancy, I had time to think – think hard about my future and that of my child. As soon as he was born, I went back to work within a week and gave Tyson to my mother to look after him during the day. Don't be surprised. By this time Grandpa Clement was living with my mom and dad and my father had mellowed from his arrogant ways quite a bit. Besides, Tyson was a boy – the boy my mother never gave him – and he did take care of him. He never lifted a hand against him. Meanwhile, he had become a business man of sorts – a drug dealer of note. He was getting wealthier and both mom and dad had slowly climbed the steps to earning a more comfortable living.

Having the added responsibility of caring for a child, I decided to further my education and raise my son the way he needed to be raised. Since I didn't have my high school Grade 12 Certificate and only the equivalent, but I was old enough to take an entry exam, I decided to tackle college. I had to quit the coffee truck because of the long hours and feeling extremely tired after Tyson's birth. Getting up at 4:00am and not finishing work until 8:00pm then having to come home and be up all night with an infant baby was not cutting it anymore. Yet, I had to find money to pay my tuition fees and other student expenses. In the meantime, I found an apartment in the *low-income housing complex and accepted to go on social assistance, which enabled me to attend school. I managed the first tuition all right but the rest was iffy going. I needed to find a job that would allow me to pay for school and care for my son. I wanted to be a mother first and foremost. I heard through friends in college that the local nightclubs had bikini contests throughout the week around what they called "the bar circuit," which paid $100 for first prize, $75 for second and $50 for third place. If I could win these contests it would help support my child while I got an education. Since I was a very attractive girl, although I had no boobs to speak of and I was good on my feet, I won many of these contests – no problem – but that wasn't all these contests did for me. They awaken the dancer in me. I loved dancing. I later became a very avid country and western dancer. Yet, I still needed a steady paycheck, and that happened when I got hired as a "strip-o-gram" girl for one of the companies in town. It was harmless enough but quite competitive and very elegant in those days. I would go to a birthday or stag party, strip down to the bare-minimum of lingerie and garters and dance a few bars to the delight of the guys and hosts.*

Still I had dancing on the brain. I looked through the classifieds and found a position at a club – they were looking for a "dancer & stripper." Back then, you didn't just wrap yourself around a pole, enticing the guy to put some money in your straps, you had to dance and be altogether elegant, poised and attractive about it. You were not flaunting your body at the drooling males gawking at you – it was all in the art of attracting attention to your curves and the beauty of your dancing. We had elaborate costumes and went in various pole competitions. Back in those days, the dancers knew how to dance and we danced hard. And from that day onward I didn't look back. Within months I rose to the top and became the "headliner feature dancer" of the place. "Brittney Fox" was my stage name. I also won several pole talent contests while working the circuit and the stage-floors. Not only was I earning good money again, but I was able to pay for my schooling. I guess, in a weird way, it gave me a false sense of security and boosted my self-esteem, but for the wrong reasons.

8.

While Simon was reading Tania's diaries, Judge Hendrix ferreted out some more information regarding Tania's previous relationships. This brought him back to reading one of her more recent journals – the only one he had kept away from Simon.

Tania Fiolleau

He wanted to read what Tania had to say about the men in her life. He wanted to set aside what he had heard during the trial. In order for him to make an impartial decision about the children's future, he needed to look at both fathers individually and at their particular relationship with Ms. Fiolleau. He knew the father of her first child had not participated in the boy's upbringing, but he also knew that the father of her second child had been involved in marring the psychological development of Tania's first son. Now it was time to look at Tania's first husband – the second man in her life.

One night at a club, I was introduced to a gorgeous guy. He was muscle-bound; at least 325 pounds bone dry, 6' 2" and with what appeared to be good manners. His name was Mike. I told my girlfriend there and then, "I will marry him!" She would not believe me, of course, but, lo and behold, in the end I did.

The whole time I was with Dwayne, he was training at a gym that Mike owned. It was the best gym in town – the gym where all the big boys trained. Dwayne wasn't aware of the fact at the time and kept talking about this "huge" guy, "You should see this guy, he's a real stud.

Souled Out

He's really got it all," he used to say. I didn't put two and two together that he was talking about Mike then.

Mike was so handsome and such a novelty, being a man of that size, with such a body that he turned heads walking down the street, I was very proud to be the one who had nabbed him out of his temporary celibacy. He had 24-inch arms, a 58-inch chest and bench pressed over 700lbs. He was a true genetic freak! However, behind the façade of gentleness lay a demon that I was to awake and of which I was to feel and endure the rage. He was a man of power—a power of doing evil while he would bestow his sadistic fury upon my son and me.

Being a single mom and living in a low-income housing then, I had been attracted to him for more than just being the "Hunk" that he was. I was attracted to the potential security of not having to struggle anymore. He drove a top of the line Corvette convertible, made some $60 an hour and maintained a plush apartment in one of the best neighborhoods in the city. But most important to me was that he appeared to accept Tyson and the fact that I was a single-mom. I wouldn't have accepted to have a brute near my little boy, had I known who he really was.

The first months of our relationship were easy enough until I noticed a jealous streak in him raise its ugly head. He wanted to have me near him always and he wanted to keep me from my friends and family. He wanted to pay the bills – not only share in the expenses, but pay for everything. I was reluctant because that would mean losing my independence and I couldn't abide even the thought of being controlled by anyone. He was slowly isolating me, which is the first sign of an abuser, but I didn't see it at the time.

Mike was sent on assignment to Prince Rupert. That's when I broke down and accepted to visit him up north. That proved to be one of the worst decisions in my life. Since he had us under his thumb then, he shed the mask of politeness and decent behavior soon after we arrived. He began yelling at Tyson and being more than rough on me. I was laid up with a vicious flu for days and he began flaring up at every thing I did or say. He screamed and yelled at me as I rolled back and forth, sick and in pain. The noise I was making was interfering with his sleep and he wanted rest to body-build at the gym. I found out that he was a steroid abuser and would take his "roid rage" out on my son and me. The second time I went up for a visit, it went from bad to worse, until one evening when we got back from a party; he was back-fisting me from the driver seat and I was kicking him to defend myself with my back against the door. He then

Souled Out

stopped the truck to the side of the road, got out, came round to the passenger side and pulled me out by my hair. He then proceeded to choke me until I was unconscious. The whole time I was scared, as you can imagine. The monster had emerged from his cave. All I could see around me were the black mountains etched against a moonlit sky. It was cold and that cold seemed to translate into shivers of terror traveling through my mind and body. I couldn't think of anything else but what would happen to Tyson if I died.

When he carried me back to the apartment, he locked me in for two long days. He called in sick for work and stayed with me, guarding me in case I would go to the authorities. When I had to go to the bathroom he would not let me close the door for fear that I would escape through the window, and he would watch me go to the bathroom. His abusive comments didn't stop, neither did his menaces. He didn't care that I could have died at his hand, no; all he cared about was that I wouldn't go out and start ratting on him.

While I dated Dwayne, I met a friend of his by the name of Wayne and we became friends. When I met Mike, Wayne was reticent – he clearly didn't like Mike. In fact, when I asked him to walk me down the aisle, he refused and never showed up at the wedding. Wayne *was a God-fearing man and still is to this day. He could not come to my wedding and condemn me for marrying Mike. I was upset at the time but I understand why today.*

Wayne had been right. All the way through our relationship, Mike manipulated my mind, my emotions and my behavior into believing that I was worthless and ugly, and with a child I couldn't be appreciated by anyone else. He would tell me, "You're just a hole to cum in. You're nothing but a vile and disgusting pig. You cellulite ass; why don't you go jiggle some more." These were just a few comments that have scarred me for life. Again, I didn't see the forest for the tree. He wanted to control and own me. Although I had been trained by the best – my father – to know what men could be, I settled for the worst man of the lot – a demented maniac and a sadist. I guess, in a sense, I thought it was normal. I grew up with this type of behavior. In a sick way, I thought if I were being abused or beaten that I was recognized. Perhaps even cared about or acknowledged.

Yet, times were not all bad with Mike. As any battered women would tell you, the men who suffer from abusive and uncontrollable rage toward their mates come begging for forgiveness more often than not. I can hardly count the times I went to a women's shelter to save myself and

Souled Out

my boy from the evil that engulfed our relationship. We all go back to them and try to believe that these demons personified would change, but they don't. I don't think I ever convinced myself that Mike would change, and what drove me back to him every time was the fear I had of him taking reprisals against me. The way he described them would have my stomach lurched in horror. He said he would pour Draino into my vagina and let me suffer the pains of hell for an entire day. Then he would cut my fingers one by one to prevent anyone from matching my finger prints, and finally he would put the barrel of a gun in my mouth to finish the job, so there wouldn't be any dental recognition possible. He said that, ultimately, he would leave me to rot in some shallow grave where no one would find me. He broke my nose and spat in my face on many occasions. One time he picked me up over his head, threw me up in the air and down the stairs where I lay, out of wind, with my lower back cracked on the bottom step. I am permanently disabled with a bad back from the injuries he inflicted upon me. In pain, I was unable to move. He ran to the bottom of the step and straddled me, laughing at me, only to spit on me. I still suffer from these injuries today. All of this, in the presence of my son, Tyson. This was one of the many assaults Mike perpetrated against me.

Tania Fiolleau

However, during one of the lulled periods of fabricated happiness, I managed to get pregnant. Again my Catholic upbringing came into play in this instance. I had been to catechism and I had strong Christian beliefs. Although I didn't always live like I had one, I had a conscience. I had given birth to one boy out of wedlock and I had sworn I would not repeat the mistake – I decided to marry the man I began to loathe by then. I figured, if nothing else, my second child would enjoy the spoils of having a well-to-do man as a father. If it didn't work out, at least I could tell Michael I did the right thing and married his father. What was I thinking?

Oh yes, Mike was highly regarded around town. He had a steady job, drove a nice car and as far as everyone was concerned, his girlfriend (me) had no want for anything. He was literally known to many as "the gentle giant" and to many he was also known for carrying out some debt collections in the past and beating up the toughest bouncers all at once at the bar, or taking out a whole rugby team in a fit of rage; he was regarded as a man of power and of some wealth. Among other assets, he owned a huge, beautiful "cabin" backing up onto the golf course of the Westwood Plateau. A prestigious part of town.

Two weeks before my wedding to Mike, he laid another beating on me. I wanted to cancel the whole thing but there was the issue of having two children from two fathers, and being unwed as well. I didn't have the nerve to call anyone and tell them the wedding was off. When they would ask why, I wouldn't have dared tell anybody. Not all of them would have believed me. They hadn't seen that side of Mike. All of that set aside, I also remained deliberately oblivious to the fact that Mike had been married before and that his wife had taken a restraining order against him.

Mike begged me not to cancel the wedding. It was a beautiful sunny day, but the second I walked down the aisle, I could see black clouds moving rapidly in the direction of the gazebo where the ceremony was held. They came fast, heavy, gloomy clouds, and tons of rain came pouring down hard right then and there. I knew it was a sign from God but I ignored it. The clouds were literally chasing me as I walked down the aisle. Two out of three of our groomsmen have died to date – one took his own life.

On our wedding night I looked very beautiful and I was in very good physical shape. I wore gorgeous white lingerie and garter set. When I took off my wedding dress I was afraid for Mike to look at my body in the lingerie, because I was scared he would say something demeaning and cruel to me, and hurt my feelings once again. How sad is that? That should have been a memorable moment where I wanted to please my husband, but instead I feared how he would degrade and belittle me.

Besides being an obvious physical tyrant, the man lured me into believing I was worthless not being able to do better than him, increasing his control over me day after day. He had no intention of seeing me go back to the club, even before Michael was born – within months of us being together. I was not to be showing myself half-naked to anyone but him – of course. Although I wanted to accumulate a college education, Mike couldn't see me going to work anywhere. Again, he wanted me to stay home and be at his disposal and under his devilish control all the time. I decided to become a stay-at-home mom against my better judgment. As Mike would say, "What kind of a mother has a kid and puts it in daycare to let someone else raise it?" I truly wanted to work but to face Mike's wrath if I did, simply wasn't worth it. Mike was adamant about it. To achieve the type of seclusion he wanted for his wife and his two sons – although he never considered Tyson as his own – he bought a spacious modular home and had it transported on a fifty-five-acre property at the outskirts of town. He set the house far away from the road at the end of a half-a-mile drive. He had it all planned. Our seclusion was complete – or so he thought. He was at liberty to abuse any of us to his heart content without any of us being able to alert the neighbors – there were none. Nobody would be able to hear or see us for miles.

Staying at home with the boys, I didn't mind being alone for the hours he spent at work. At night, however, all I wanted was to escape my husband's clutches. I took up country and western dancing and involved myself in community activities as much as I possibly could, which would see me out of the house once a week for a couple of hours. As I mentioned before, I loved dancing. I also got involved with people who had horses and we would go riding together on occasions. This infuriated Mike. He didn't want me to have any friends.

Mike didn't believe in God. He had absolutely no desire to be involved with anything remotely religious. He was a true atheist. He made my life a living hell anytime I tried to go to church, let alone take his son to a service. Unfortunately, one of the people I met who had a fondness for horses, such as I did, was a very religious person. Mike saw another opportunity to create dissension between me and this girl and to reproach my liking her – because she was a church-goer.

I had another friend, by the name of Rebecca, who was also banned from the house. Rebecca could tell you how much I suffered at the hands of the monster. I knew her since I was 17 and she witnessed some horrific demonstrations of Mike's sadism. Mind you, she remained steadfast and she's still a very dear friend to this day, although we don't talk much anymore.

He tried isolating me from anyone who was not only close to me but who was a Christian. Among those, I counted Grandma Alma, Rebecca, of course, and Wayne, in particular.

While I was away either riding or going to my country dancing classes, Mike would enjoy playing evil games

Souled Out

with my son, Tyson. My little tyke would try to show me what he did to him when I was away, but at such a young age he was incapable of explaining what he felt or endured at the hands of his step-father.

Michael

A couple of games of choice were the times when he got his little nephew to place fire crackers in Tyson's ears and told him to light them – but I caught him just in time. Or, he would insert battery-ends in Tyson's mouth telling him they were candies, and then he would make him cry so that the child would get an electrical shock. I was blind and ignorant to this until an aunt of mine, who was a nurse, brought to my attention that he was doing something to Tyson. Tyson would refuse to go back with Mike when it came time to going home with him. She knew the signs. She had seen abused children before. Tyson would claw my mom's neck and scream and cry, "No daddy Mike! No daddy Mike!"

Mike even went as far as putting an elastic band around the boy's penis, cutting off his circulation, angered because Tyson cried like a baby. My mom took Tyson to the doctor because his scrotums had swollen up the size of grapefruits and we didn't know what the matter was. The doctor told her what might have happened. That's what hurt me the most. This beast hurt my son – that was more damaging to me than anything else.

When the boy was lured into believing that some affection was at hand, Mike would call him, making him believe he was to give him a hug, and then shove his foot in Tyson's stomach, which kicked him through the window opposite his chair. Other times, he would call him to give him a kiss and when Tyson was about a foot from him, Mike would see fit to spit at the little boy's face.

Souled Out

Tyson was so young and trusting, he was just hoping for once he would receive a kiss and some love from this man, only to be lured into getting his face spat on or physically injured.

Coming home one evening from the country-dance club – in the middle of November – I found Tyson in his diaper, shivering in front of the door on the porch. Under the pretext that the poor little boy was crying too much, Mike had decided to put him outside to cool him off and had told him the coyotes would eat him – those were his words to Tyson – and Mike admitted it as well. Besides being in danger to catch a deadly chill, my husband had deliberately put the child outside – a prey for the roaming coyotes around the property – in the pitch black with the porch light off, in the cold and being told the coyotes were going to eat him.

No one would wonder why there were so many coyotes around the property. Mike would buy 50lb bags of dog food and dump them behind the house where Tyson would play. He told me it was because the coyotes were hungry.... No one in their right mind would feed coyotes around one's property unless they really wanted trouble. When I now think about it, he probably wanted to lure them to the house where Tyson would play and be in easy reach to be attacked.

Tania Fiolleau

I promptly flew into a rage. I ran to the kitchen, grabbed a knife and menaced him with it. I had a good mind to kill him. All that I had suffered at the hands of my father came back – the memories were driving me ever closer to the brink of despair. I wanted to kill him! I wanted to make him pay for the deceit, for the sadism that had shown behind that veil of kindness, but most of all, the hatred I had developed for men in general was gearing my thoughts and my words if not my knife yet. In my eyes, he saw a vengeance that could not be tamed. He saw that I meant to kill him without regard for the consequences. And for the first time, perhaps in his entire life, Mike felt scared. He ran to his bedroom, locked the door and brought every piece of furniture in front of it, making sure he would hear me coming at him through the night if he happened to fall asleep. Calming down ever so slightly, I went to my son, tucked him in and fell asleep beside his bed – the knife at my side.

Apart from abusing Tyson, Mike continued applying pressure on me. He needed me to stay the subservient wife I had become. He would have me believe I looked ugly. He used to tell me how his previous wife had a way prettier face than mine. One night he came home, came to the bathroom and asked me why I was putting make up

Souled Out

on. I replied, "Because I am a girl and that's what girls do."

He said, "You couldn't put enough make up on that face to make it pretty."

This is the sort of things that lowers your self-esteem, degrades you and kills your desire to be anything else than what your mate wants you to be. Although he never touched a hair on Michael's head, he didn't spare the abuse on me or Tyson.

I tried to shut the bathroom door, so I wouldn't have to look at his face. He then grabbed me by the hair and threw me into the bathtub and slammed my head against the faucet, and repeated the slamming of my skull against it until I was bleeding profusely – all of which he made sure happened in front of Tyson. While I was laying in the tub wounded and bleeding, he chased Tyson out of the bathroom in a rage, threatening him for trying to help his mommy, only to come back a few minutes later to pee all over my body and face and around the tub. Can you even fathom how humiliating that sort of thing would feel? Then he said, "You can go now," in a laughing, demented, satisfied, sarcastic way.

Yet that wasn't all. Mike had a grand-plan – even before we moved into the modular home. He wanted to have me declared an un-fit mother and take away

Michael from me. He wanted to build a case against me. As for Tyson, I don't think he cared whether he lived or died. He knew someone would call 911 every time. So, he would turn the tables on me for the benefits of the cops who came knocking. I'll give you an example. Mike bought some marijuana for fishing. Since I was fourteen, I had not touched an ounce of dope or even smoked anything. Having dope in the house sent me in a revolting mood. And that's what Mike wanted all along – another fight. After he had slapped me around a couple of times, the neighbor called the cops, worried I was getting hurt and when they came to the door, Mike told them that I was a dumb stripper who brought dope to our home.... He would do such things at every opportunity, so that the social services would begin to believe his tread-bare stories. Thank goodness that at times the police were smarter than this devil. They had seen through his game – I had the scars to prove it and still do to this day.

The assaults were many and not very far apart unfortunately. Each time, I would try to run for the phone to call 911, but he would rip the cord out of the wall before I could get to it. However, during one of his demented fits, I managed to call 911. Although he weighed 325 pounds, he had the agility of an ape. Before I could pronounce the first words, he grabbed the receiver

Souled Out

out of my hand and went from Mr. Jackal to Mr. Hyde, calmly telling them to get an ambulance, to come get me for I took a bunch of pills and tried to kill myself. He then fetched some pills from the bathroom, grabbed me by the throat and physically forced me to swallow all of the tablets. I tried not to, but I was no match for him. When the ambulance and police arrived, he remained all calm, acted like the loving, caring husband and father, telling them I went nuts and swallowed a bunch of pills with the kids in the house. I denied it and tried to explain the truth, but all the paramedics and officers saw was that I was the distraught one (not Mike) and that I was the one who had attempted suicide. He grinned at me and laughed as they took me away on a stretcher when the police and paramedics weren't looking. So, off in the ambulance I went and Mike stayed home with my two sons. I worried for Tyson.

There were more insults, more abuse, more maneuvers to have me declared unfit, suicidal or whatever he felt was a more hurtful device or plan to get rid of me in some ways. As for me, I had enough. I had to get out from under his oppressive and sadistic control. Moreover, I wanted my son, Tyson, and even Michael, to get out of this infernal atmosphere. Tyson was growing up and I couldn't bear the thought of having him endure more traumatic experiences such as the injury he received when Mike directed his dirt bike onto the tailgate of his truck. All excited to be allowed to ride one of the bikes owned by one of Mike's nephews, Tyson revved it on Mike's instruction, trusting his intentions were good, unaware of the speed at which the bike would take off. In less than a second he smashed into the obstacle. We were living in the modular home by then and I was watching out the window not realizing what he was instructing Tyson to do. He pointed the bike towards the back of the pick-up truck, purposely putting the tailgate down so it was at the same level as Tyson's face, and then directed my son to pull the throttle to have his face smashed in the tailgate. Again, my husband could have killed him. There were literally miles of property around the driveway onto which Mike could have shown the boy how to handle the bike, but, no, he chose to have Tyson run into the open tail-gate of the pick-up, so the boy would be hurt. He did it on purpose!

As the months passed, I slowly went down into a deep depression. Recalling how Silver had once offered such consolation for my suffering when I was a little girl, I bought a small gelding. He was a beautiful horse. His name was Brody but I called him "Little Bamby Dear"

Souled Out

because of his patches of brown and white that reminded me of a deer.

The boys were still young...

Tania Fiolleau

He was six months old when I got him. I grew such an attachment to Brody that I would spend countless hours with him out at the barn just as I did with Silver when I was very young. Mike saw and knew how much I loved Brody. Whenever we would fight and I would threaten to leave him, he would menace to put antifreeze in Brody's water trough. One time Brody became ill with extreme colic and he almost died. To this day I believe that Mike put antifreeze in Brody's water as the vet even told me he ingested something poisonous.

On another occasion, I did leave Mike, and I hid Brody in a neighboring field for fear that Mike would hurt him in retaliation against me. I was right. I went out to the field to find Brody's hind leg slashed in long and deep cuts. Mike suggested it was a cougar, but there were no cougars that would dare come to the herds of horses in the field. The vet said that it was clear that Brody had been slashed with a knife. Even after all that, Mike had the nerve to try to take my horse in the divorce settlement, claiming it was half his. Knowing he would eventually kill him, I hid the horse for years, making Mike believe it had been stolen.

Mike continued to be manipulative and be sadistically abusive until I saw an opportunity to get away.

9.

Meanwhile, Judge Hendrix had asked Simon to look into Ms. Fiolleau's ability to work for a living! Which statement had taken Simon aback; the woman had demonstrated time and again that she had fought to survive, so what was in the judge's mind? Simon decided to ask for an explanation one evening when they were spending some time at the judge's favorite club.

"Alright, what's on your mind? You've been brewing all day...."

"Well, sir, you've asked me to see whether Ms. Fiolleau would be able to earn a living if she got custody of the kids...." Judge Hendrix nodded. "But I thought that was obvious enough..."

"Let me stop you right there, Simon. Ms. Fiolleau has endeavored to earn a living – I grant you that – but in what field – in an industry that she promised to leave if (or when) we give her custody of the children. Besides which, we know she held a job with the ferries, but we also know that she needed to leave that professional endeavor when she entered the escort business. On the other hand, we also know that she is currently in a third relationship – her second marriage – and the only thing that keeps that family afloat right now is Ms. Fiolleau's earnings through prostitution. In view of these facts, what I want to ascertain is that once she leaves the industry with four mouths to feed – how will she cope? Will she be forced by circumstances, once again, to earn money through the brothels' revenue? Or is there something that will induce me to believe she could make it on her own?"

This whole statement put Simon on the defensive. "But, sir, if she gets full custody of her two sons, couldn't she go back to the ferries, or continue studying...?"

"No, Simon." The Judge shook his head. "Although, I'm sure she could go back to university or acquire further education, but I have my doubts as to her ability to find a job that will feed the family. And don't forget that she is now an invalid resulting from being thrown down the stairs and from the beatings she suffered at the hands of her first husband."

"Okay, I guess, I better see what I can find out...."

"You do that, and then it will be time to make a decision."

That night, Simon didn't sleep – he spend quite a few hours reading and making notes as to the possible answers to the Judge's question: How will Ms. Fiolleau manage to feed her family once she quit the industry?

Souled Out

He decided to return to another of Tania's journal where she explained how she got out of her first husband's clutches and was forced into the prostitution industry.

As I said, I had enough – more than enough – I wanted out. I had to protect Tyson. However, to get out I needed to find work and earn a living to support not only my two boys but me as well, not to mention live in a safe place.

At the time, we lived quite close to the Albion ferry run and the thought of working on one of these vessels appealed to me. It represented freedom. Being on the water, however short the voyage would be, would give me a sense of being away from it all while earning a living that would enable me to raise the boys properly. I really enjoyed talking with all the passengers and petting the horses and dogs they would bring across on sunny days.

Of course, the problem was to get out from under Mike's constant vigil. Nevertheless, I applied for a position with the ferries but was told that I would have to take courses in order to step into the job. There were several courses to take and months of training to attend. I had no choice – it was either that or staying home. Since I wanted the job, I took the courses and the training and re-applied. Although a female, and not tall or muscular as some – or as most guys are on the ferry runs – I was hired as an auxiliary deckhand. However, there were many more of these courses to take and several more months and sea-hours had to pass before I could reach the grade of First Mate. I had to complete all of the courses and get in my sea-time. You have to have a certain amount of accumulated hours on the water before you could advance to mate position, not to mention an additional six-month course at the Pacific Marine Training Institute. I actually wanted to get to the top – I imagined myself being the captain of one of these vessels. Why not? I figured, I was intelligent enough, I was good at learning what needed to be learned, and within four months of being hired, I already climbed the ladder to main deckhand. The senior captain had taken me aside and offered to have the Ministry of Transportation and Highways put me through school to become a captain one day. Others, with much more seniority than I ever had, stood by and watched me go up the ranks quicker than they had – if they had at all. I was studying and working hard. The senior captain himself was helping me with my chart work. I enjoyed the water so much that years later, I bought a beautiful boat. The senior captain chose to put me through the schooling over seamen that had been

Souled Out

there for over 25 years. I got the top academic mark in my marine firefighting course out of 30 men in my class. Me being the only woman! They gave me my own florescent pink hat instead of the florescent orange one the other men were wearing.

But all of this didn't go down without effort on the "home" front. A home that didn't exist anymore anyway. I had left Mike and gone into a shelter with the boys again, after another beating (too many to count, really) and had stayed there until I had made enough money to get into

an apartment. It took me approximately seventeen times of fleeing domestic violence before I made the final break. Back then they said the average woman would leave seven times before making the final break. The social services told me that if I didn't leave for good, I could lose my babies for they would not allow young children to be witnessing that type of abuse anymore. I was so afraid every time I left him. I was so afraid of what would happen to Tyson and me should I go back.

The people at the shelter suggested that I changed my appearance and died my hair blond so that Mike would have a hard time finding me amid the crowd. In a few weeks, I was transformed. I had blond hair; I had bought an old beat up motor bike to run around town and to go from the ferries to the courses or the training centre – or to run whatever errands I had to run. Before I bought the bike, I had to hitch-hike and this was a very terrifying thing for me to do again, believe me. I was so afraid, I prayed constantly for God to keep me safe until I could get that bike. With a full face motorcycle helmet it would be hard for him to recognize me. People did not recognize me, but Mike did. Oh yes! It didn't work. Whether he had someone follow me or whether he saw me somewhere and put two and two together, it didn't take

Souled Out

him long to chase me and to run me down. And I mean that literally.

It occurred on a country road just outside of town. I was coming down one way; he was coming down the other. I tried avoiding him or passing him somehow, but he kept blocking my way with his work van, until I had to stop. He got out of the truck and yelled, "Why did you dye your hair blonde!? You're back working as a stripper!" He always liked blondes. I was blonde when I met him as a dancer. However, when I settled down with him, I went back to brunette – my natural color. For me to go back to blonde set him off in a fury. He got in the truck and reversed the pick-up and to my complete surprise and disbelief, he floored the gas pedal and ran straight at me. I was thrown off my bike before I knew what was happening, with the wind knocked right out of me. Yet, it was not enough for him. I was on the ground, injured, lying in pain and he did nothing other than reverse the truck once again and run over me. What's worse, he did this while Michael was in the truck watching his mother being run over. The memory of my son's face screaming in fear, as he watched his mother being plowed down will be forever carved in my memory. When he was assured that I didn't move, he sped off and disappeared, but not before someone had seen what he had done, took his license plate number and phoned 911. The police immediately put out an APB alert on him and he was soon arrested and charged.

In hospital, the diagnosis wasn't the best but not the worst either. I had injuries that eventually ran from permanent to not so serious. I believe my guardian angel had watched over me and I recovered somehow. My lower tailbone was cracked and I had two herniated disks. The damage to my back never healed completely. Today, the pain is still there – latent – a permanent reminder that Mike had mangled my body for life. I also developed fibro-myalgia since then, which is worsening each year. It causes me intense pain, lack of energy and low moods. I now suffer from debilitating, permanent migraine headaches. I will never be the woman I once was. But, and again, thank God, I am alive.

Mike was (and still is) a very jealous man. He couldn't admit defeat. He had to avenge my departure. He had to take reprisals against me because I was proving him wrong – I had a job and I was making it on my own – without him.

Since the police were able to trace him down, he was arrested and tried for assault. He should have been charged with hit-and-run and child endangerment also. He needed to make me pay – of course! Can you believe it? After the trial and now his third conviction for abusing me, he paid the fine – $500, one year probation and ordered to take a course in anger management. He even got kicked out of the anger management program due to being too angry and uncooperative.

Nevertheless, this time, I was not going back. I was not going to let him have my sons, especially Tyson, and I wasn't going to back down. I wanted a divorce and I wanted custody of the boys. Mike threatened me, saying that no judge would separate the boys or give them to a "nut-bar" like me, and he'd get them both. He would threaten me that once he got custody of Tyson that the boy was "going to get it!" He actually never referred to the children by their names but referred to each of them as "the boy."

To go into court and plead for custody when your ex-husband is a wealthy and respected member of the community is not a mean feat even in spite of his convictions. Remember, he had paved the way for me to be considered as an unfit mother, a psychotic, a suicidal maniac and or whatever else he would be trying to prove in court in order to be awarded sole custody of both children. He had financial stability and a stable, high-paying job in which he had remained for many years. I *needed a lawyer and a good one. Yet, lawyers – good ones – don't come cheap. The one I had been recommended would accept to take my case if I paid him a $5000 retainer immediately with more to follow. I applied for legal-aid but was turned down due to having a government job and my name on our marital home. Although I was working as an auxiliary, my hours weren't stable, nor would my wages even cover daycare or my mortgage. I was already in the hole. Where would I get five thousand dollars overnight practically, to engage his services? The lawyer gave me the advice that if I didn't hire a lawyer I might as well tie my own noose. That question had not many answers and one of them came in the form of answering an ad asking for "girls to work in a massage parlor." It was an alluring ad and it promised to pay good money very quickly. It promised a friendly, fun, safe working environment with the assurance of earning up to $1500 a day. The ad also mentioned that it was a female-owned and operated enterprise. That's all I needed, but I had no idea what "to work in a massage parlor" meant. Maybe I was naïve, maybe I didn't want to admit what the possibilities were, but all I cared about at that moment was to win custody of the boys – nothing else mattered. I couldn't fathom the idea of the children witnessing Mike abusing his next*

Souled Out

wife as he did me. I couldn't fathom the idea of Tyson being continuously tortured by him and there wouldn't be a thing I could do about it. It simply wasn't going to happen! Mama bear was backed in a corner and her claws came out! She was going to do anything to protect her cubs! Anything!

When I got to the appointment, I was surprised, to say the least. Not only was it a beautifully appointed brothel, well decorated, and the "girls" that were working there were all gorgeous. Top of the class models, tall and elegant – I really felt like the runt of the litter to tell you the truth. But I couldn't let my self-conscious attitude ruin the day. I decided I was as beautiful as they were, and I felt certainly a lot smarter than they were. I was going to beat them at whatever game they were playing – no two ways about it. Besides, I needed the money.

A couple of hours (days) later, I was facing my first appointment – I went to it and through it without seeing or feeling anything. Somehow I had shielded myself from any thought that would deter me from my goal – $5,000 to retain my lawyer. The first night I made $1,700. Yet that wasn't enough. I needed five thousand – for a start – and more later. So, I asked the manager to book me for "a double" again and then another. I soon developed a sense of what this "escort" business was all about. Men *of all sorts wanted to spend an hour with a woman who would have sex with them and then dismiss them until the next time round. It would have been simple enough if it had not been for the emotional scarring each encounter would involve unless I could scrape my body from the shame and repulsive dirt these fellows left on me.*

I remember the first night; I literally brushed myself raw in the shower. I broke down sobbing. I lost all of my physical strength and just shrank to the bottom corner of the shower. The water poured over me as I cried and scrubbed my skin. I could not get clean enough. I could not divest myself of the memory of the man's face – until I shut it out of my mind. I could not explain to you how I did it, but perhaps, the mere idea that if I didn't do this, I would lose my boys kept me going. I kept telling myself, "I'm doing it for the boys. I'm doing it for my boys." Little did I know that down the road this wicked disease would affect and scar them, too. I was just so beaten down emotionally by Mike that he had me convinced I was a basket case and no judge in his right mind would let me keep my sons.

This one girl at the brothel told me on my first day when I asked her how the girls mentally coped with doing it – she said, "I am a robot and I block it all out.

Souled Out

And a piece of advice; never ever look the 'John' in the eyes as he is having sex with you. It will destroy you."

One time a 'John' made me look him in the eyes. He demanded that I do while he had sex and use my body. I will admit it took a huge part of me to do that.

The weeks passed and I gave myself to more and more "Johns" without thinking twice about it anymore. I began amassing money and material possessions, but I had no credit reference (again) to allow me to buy a car. One of the other escorts then referred me to a car-lot owner who was apparently willing to front the car for me so that I could pay him on installments and finally end up owning the car at the other end of the deal. He was a Persian gangster and he dealt with gangsters on international levels. He gave these types of loans to all the shady people that made good money illegitimately. This little transaction opened another door for me. In fact, the owner had a car lot but he also owned and managed another two brothels. Well, it didn't take him long to offer me the management of one of the brothels and I went at it all heartedly. Perhaps this is the wrong way to describe my attitude at the time – I no longer had a heart. I had divorced myself from all of it. I had become a "madam" and I had girls to do the work for me, but I think what struck most people who knew me then was that I had become ruthless. I was not the same anymore. Other veteran escorts in the business didn't like the fact that this young girl, who was new to the business, was now a madam and was running Sam's brothel. I treated all of my girls fairly but there were no valid excuse for them not to go to a rendezvous. Some of them would tell me they would not go to an appointment on Sunday because they went to church.... My response was always the same, "You're a whore and you want to go to church?" I ran it like a military boot camp and the girls hated it. But they soon realized that they were now making a lot of money and stopped complaining amongst each other about my management tactics.

I disrespected the work, I hated the men who stooped to have their jollies with any female just because they were "beautiful," and I continued to ignore the path on which I was now traveling. I needed more and more money, if I were to win the court case. Besides, it felt good to be respected even if the respect was deemed justified and often not earned. Truth be told, I had lost respect for myself and I didn't care what others thought of me. I wanted to be the best in my trade and I knew I could. I got that brothel running very successfully and then Sam put me onto the other brothel to get that one up and going as well. In fact, when I took over the second parlor, it was considered the first "grand-father" of all brothels in town. At the time it had been there for 25 years, but it made the least money. I turned that around so fast; that veteran madams in the trade had a hard time believing Madam Nina could do this so quickly. I had converted it into a successful brothel for the first time in twenty-five years when every other previous owner could not even afford to keep the doors open. We were a couple suburbs away from the downtown core and I was beating out the busiest brothel numbers in the city. The other madams were asking the girls, "Who the hell is this Nina?"

While I was well on my way to turn things around at the first brothel, the owner got himself arrested and was soon on his way to a twenty-five year sentence for murder in the first degree. Seeing that no one would be there to watch over his businesses for a long while, he asked me if I'd be interested in purchasing the second brothel – the grandfather of all brothels – and that he would financially carry me for part of the purchase price. This was an offer I could not refuse. That was the sort of challenge that appealed to me. However, I didn't know how much of a challenge it was going to be. The girls that were employed at that parlor were 'hardcore'. They were 'street prostitutes' who would fetch their 'Johns' at the corner of the street in the evenings or anywhere they found someone ready to pay for the service after hours when the brothel was closed. These were tough chicks. I soon realized I was nobody to them – a stranger among them; someone who knew nothing about being a madam, (or so they thought). If I wanted to acquire their respect, I needed to assert my presence and make decisions that would not only encourage them to stay with me but also deter them from continuing to offer their trade in the street. I had to polish them up, yet keep them off the street. If I was going to own a brothel it had to be a brothel that had the classiest, most beautiful service providers, and that provided the best service around.

In the first parlor, I had asked for Sam's assistance in that regard. He couldn't do anything himself, but he alerted his cohorts of his predicament and asked a well-feared motorcycle gang to lend him a hand in seeing that I was well protected or 'appreciated' in my endeavors. So, it didn't take long for three or four guys to show up on the front steps and make sure the girls knew who they would be dealing with if anything went wrong, or if their behavior was not up-to-par. He also sent a huge, well-known Russian assassin, whom would later become my second husband.

Souled Out

As I mentioned before, I was fair and I cared very much what happened to these girls, but I was not to be trampled on either. The second day I was at the second parlor, I decided that if I wanted to introduce new rules in the place I had better fire everyone and ask them to re-apply for the position. That was going to give me the opportunity to interview each woman separately and evaluate whether they would make the cut or not in their new surroundings.

One of the girls, a young, black woman would have none of it. She wanted to stay where she was and she wanted to remain in control. I knew the reason for this attitude; she had a pimp and she was a thief, taking from the business when Sam owned it. She had the run of the place. If she didn't comply with her pimp's wishes (rather than mine) she would face a serious beating. She was a tall, thick-built woman that was a hardcore working girl from the track. Although I understood the reasons behind her reaction to my firing her, I needed to show "who was boss" around the place, before she would be allowed to set foot in the brothel again. Yet I was somewhat intimidated by her. Yes, she scared me. She was a feisty woman. I had no desire to fight with her, but when it came to blows, I wanted to maintain the upper hand. Amid the screams and the yelling and her trying to *intimidate me, she decided to try to get the better of me and advanced towards me menacingly. I had to do something. I was afraid she would go to the kitchen drawer, take out a knife and use it on me, same as she did the week before on someone else, outside in the lane. A week before there was a police incident where she shanked another girl behind the brothel during an argument over a 'John'. I decided I needed to take her out of the way and defend myself from her demoniac assault. She was bigger and more muscular than I was, but I was in much better health than she was. We went at each other and, right away, I used some of my self-defense skills and soon got the upper hand. Perhaps the rage that came over me during the battle was a little too much for her to bear – I put her in the hospital with very serious injuries.*

The big Russian man, who had come to show his masterful presence to the girls in the previous days, had to pull me off her before I committed murder without realizing what I was doing. I blacked out and continuously beat on her while she lay lifeless and unconscious. In the end, I was glad he had come in just in time to avoid a disaster. His name was Taras. What a beautiful person he was, what a gentle soul he was – I loved him. I know it sounds odd to say he was a gentle soul, considering he was an assassin, but he truly was to the ones he loved.

But let's go back to my vicious girl for a minute. Our little interlude didn't stop there. She was taken to the hospital that night and her injuries were so severe that the doctors had to advise the police of her brutal attack. They hauled me to the station, in handcuffs, accused of assault causing bodily harm. I tell you, there have been days during my life when I have been scared out of my wits, but that night, I was beyond scared; I could see my future falling apart along with that of my boys. There was no way I could even think of getting custody of Tyson and Michael if these charges went any further than the holding cell.

I had gone too far for too long to back down now. The divorce had been final and Michael was allowed to visit his father every weekend. Mike would take him on Friday and bring him back on Sunday. Meanwhile, the court battle for me to obtain full (and sole) custody of the two boys was raging, and being accused of aggravated assault wasn't going to do anyone any good.

The Crown Counsel was the only person who would see through this muddle of accusations and would probably listened to me – ultimately dropping the charges – I hoped. I wrote to him after my release, explaining who *this girl was; the fact that she was a well-known prostitute with a dubious past; that she had a pimp, alerting him that she was known to have knifed a person in the alley at the back of the parlor and that the incident was police documented. I pleaded self-defense and lo and behold, the man actually listened to me. In hindsight, I could say he would have had little choice in the matter, but at the time, I really thought my guardian angel was looking out for me once again. He had the charges dropped and I walked out a free woman – without prejudice, and without a criminal record.*

Before taking over the management of the second brothel, I had asked Sam to have someone show "what was what" to my ex-husband. I just wanted someone more intimidating and authoritative than Mike to let him know that he couldn't put his hands on me, hurt me or threaten me in any way, shape or form and to let him know that if he did, there would be consequences. Oh yes, Mike was still being a pest. Now that he had no contact with me and that Michael was "transferred" into his temporary custody every Friday, he chose to nag and scare every nanny who would show up with his son. He would instill fear in them, menace them in some ways, so much so that one by one these poor girls would quit on me. He would frighten them any way he saw fit if they wouldn't tell him where I was living. He did this on purpose so that I would have no one to mediate transfers on the weekend. That would enable him to tell the courts that I was denying him access, creating a situation whereby he could say I was alienating Michael from him when I wasn't. Such as I said earlier, he was paving the way to make me look bad.

This intolerable atmosphere could not go on, and that's when I decided to ask for Sam's help. He said that he knew some people who would be only too glad to lend a hand.

When Taras came to the door, I practically fell over in surprise. It was the same guy that had come before to help with the girls. The same guy that pulled me off the girl I had beaten unconscious. I told you that Mike was a big man – well, Taras topped him yet again. His growling Russian accent masked a gentle soul. Imagine a grizzly with the tenderness of heart of a child's teddy bear, and you've got a perfect description of Taras. After falling in love with Taras, I found out that he was allegedly suspected of several murders and was a hit man and debt collector. A very successful one, too.

We talked for a bit before he would accept to take on the assignment of putting Mike back in his place. During our conversation, Taras told me that if Mike showed any *signs of rebellion or attacked him in some ways, he may have no choice but end up killing him, if it came to that, but that he would do everything to avoid it. My God, I thought, that's all I need – a felony murder in my hands. I didn't have to think about this for very long. I just wanted Taras to make his presence known and who he was and let it be known that the abuse must stop or else. I told Taras that his occasional protection would be good enough and that I would rather not have him approach Mike at the time.*

However, Taras had left his gentle mark on me, making it known that he was always there for me if I needed him. And he was. He stood by me through thick and thin. I was falling for the guy quicker than I even wanted to admit to myself. A year into the trial, and only six months after meeting him, saw us going down the aisle. He loved me and I loved him. This gentle giant brought peace to our home and some sort of stability through a horrid part of our lives.

When I say that Taras "jumped ship"; I mean that literally. Before we met, he arrived in Canada and obtained his landed immigrant visa. His only means of living amounted to doing "jobs" for some Russian Organizations, which will remain nameless, and other organizations as well. He was now a traitor to his home land; jumping ship and swimming a long distance to shore then hiding out until the ship left the country and claiming refugee status. If he were to go back to Russia, he would be killed there. The choice between Taras remaining in the country or being deported for being accused of shooting someone, was no choice – I didn't want to see him convicted, hauled off to jail, or being sent back to Russia, but I certainly wanted him to remain here.

I thought of marrying him primarily because I loved him but also as a way to offer him sanctuary in my country so that he wouldn't be deported back to Russia after serving time here in Canada if he were to be convicted of the crime he had been charged with.

How did I learn Taras had a racket of charges hanging over him? Let me tell you the story.

In the midst of the trouble I had with keeping nannies in my employ – Mike being scaring them at every opportunity – I needed to keep his visitation rights as my goal. Mike was looking for an excuse to sway the court's decision and if I missed to transfer Michael on any given weekend, he would have the ace to break the deck, if I were not to pick up or drop off my son. Since I was at my wits' end to find a nanny that would accept to transfer Michael on that particular weekend, and since I didn't want to do it myself for fear that Mike would hurt me again, I asked Taras to assist in the transfer for me. We were not already married at the time, and although I knew he would do anything for me, I had no idea, in how much trouble this little exercise could have cost him.

On the other hand, I didn't want to start anything between Taras and Mike. Such a confrontation would have easily turned into a blood-bath. Therefore, I thought the best place to do the transfer was in front of a police station for the safety of everyone, given Mike's violent history. If Mike would start anything, he would be nabbed right there and then for disorderly conduct, at least.

The date was set and the location agreed upon. Mike hadn't got a clue he would be handing my son to my future husband. As soon as he saw Taras get out of the car, he began yelling profanities and insults as he charged toward him. That, of course, attracted the attention of every police officer around the place. Taras only wanted to receive Michael from his father and bring him back to me where I sat watching in the car but couldn't refrain from towering over Mike when he heard all of the deprecatory remarks Mike had flaunted at his face.

Souled Out

It wasn't long until an altercation broke out between the two men. The police came rushing out from inside the station and had to intervene between these two excessively large, muscular men. As soon as I saw the whole thing was getting out of hand, I got out of the car. It was then that the police hauled everyone into the station to get to the bottom of the situation and ran all of our names. This is when an officer approached me saying, "Do you know this guy is out on bail and up on charges for a shooting and is a suspect in murders?" He was pointing to Taras.

My mouth fell open. I had not realized up to that point how dangerous Taras really was. However, I believed no matter what the circumstances were he would never hurt me or my sons. I had no answer for the man. We all then left; Taras and I got back into the car.

When Taras and I went home, and I had him between four eyes, I asked him for the truth. He hadn't told me a lie – he had not said anything about it.

Sometime later, Taras answered the charges, went through the trial, but the case was soon dismissed on a technicality.

Simon had his answer: Ms. Fiolleau would do everything necessary to feed her family. She would not return to prostitution and that for two reasons; she had suffered too much at the hands of too many men and she had the strength of character to take responsibility and make a success of any business she would choose to pursue. She had the business savvy and the 'street sense' required to be successful.

10.

Some weeks later, one night, Judge Hendrix entered Simon's office unexpectedly saying, "Okay, are you ready for it?"

"Ready for what, Your Honor?" Simon lifted his gaze to him.

"Ready to hear my decision in Ms. Fiolleau's case."

Simon was all attentive now. He had been waiting for this day for several months. Having read everything that was to be read about the case and having prepared three or more briefs in regards to the questions Judge Hendrix had posed from time to time, he was ready, indeed.

Simon smiled as the judge took a seat opposite him. "All right," Judge Hendrix began, "I have reviewed the case in its every detail, as you know, and the only decision I could render is in favor of Ms. Fiolleau."

Souled Out

The only thing Simon did was to exhale a sigh of relief. "Sir, I am grateful…"

"Why would that be, my dear boy? I know you have been quite taken by this case, but why would you be grateful?"

"Because, Your Honor, as you are aware I'm sure, this decision will set a precedent, and the courage it must have taken you to reach such a decision deserves not only my gratefulness, but my admiration."

Eyebrows arched, Judge Hendrix said, "but that does not tell me *why* you are grateful. Although I accept your gratitude, I'd like to know why you feel that way."

"Sir, while it's true that I read as much as possible about the case, as a man I felt compelled to delve into the matter of prostitution in this country. I have no idea what the future holds at this point, but I am grateful that you made such a decision because it will enable Ms. Fiolleau to participate – as she seems willing to try – into assisting the prostituted women of this world to get out of the industry."

"That's a tall order for any woman to follow, Simon. Do you think she will be up to the task?"

"Do you recall our first meeting about the case, after the trial, when you showed me the transcripts and you said, "*She has no intention to remain in the prostitution industry – and she wants to leave this ungraceful past of hers behind*"? And that told me that you believed in her, that you wanted for her not only to get out of the industry, but also fight for the girls she has hurt through prostitution. She is not going to stop at getting out of the industry; she is going to help others do the same."

Judge Hendrix smiled and nodded. "Yes, Simon, we have a plague in our hands – in our homes even – and when I had time to research the case that have passed through this court and others, and review some of the statistics that are currently available, I thought I would give Ms. Fiolleau the chance to prove that she's not only worthy to be a mother to her children, but a woman who can redress a deplorable situation."

"Would you mind if I read some of the documents you reviewed during your research, Your Honor?"

"Not at all, Simon. And if one day, we have the chance to talk to Ms. Fiolleau again, I, for one, would like to see confirmation of what I suspect she is capable of accomplishing."

Souled Out

Tania re-united with her boys

PART II
The End
and
The Beginning

11.

Right off the bat, Taras showed immense love for the children. He was there for them – day or night, they could count on Taras being at their sides. As for me, I went on with the management of the one parlor. Taras never objected to my working in such an environment. At first, I was pleased, but then it started to bug me. How could any man allow his wife to manage a brothel or being a madam? Did he really love me? He said to me one day, "Who am I to judge you? Who am I to say what you should do or not do? Who am I to prevent you from getting your children?" He had given me the freedom I needed to be who I needed to be for as long as I needed to be – a person I loathed. Yes, I loathed who I had become, but what else was there for me to do – a job that would earn me enough money to fight the monster Mike had proven to be?

Taras's work amounted to an occasional paycheck since I had made it clear that if he were staying with me, he was not to do anything that would affect my trial. That occasional paycheck, however, was not enough to support a family of four or to pay the legal fees that were piling up every day of the four plus years the trial lasted. The court proceedings went from Provincial

Court to Supreme Court. Amassing money and working long hours, I finally got enough to buy a house, engage a nanny for the children and apply myself to being a wife and mother – that's all I did during this seemingly endless battle to obtain custody of my two boys. For four long years, I continued in the sex trade for money, and ran a brothel but kept my mind in check – as much as I could. I didn't have peace, I didn't find happiness. And all wasn't fair in this war. I was so tired of it all that one night I literally crashed through the door of our home and screamed my frustration at my husband, falling to my knees to the floor, frail and emotionally spent. I was at the end of my tether, yet the end was not in sight. The children are not yet mine to keep safe.

****

As I described earlier, Taras was a beautiful man in every sense of the word. He had a heart of gold and with his trimmed hair and clean-shaven face; he hid that fierce character for being fair and open-minded well away from those he didn't know. People didn't mean anything to him. He had been raised in Russia and trained in the army. He taught the Russian soldiers combat fighting; to kill with their bare hands. He was also a trained sniper. A sharp shooter. He was a trained killer, but not one without a conscience. His character play in the movies always shows the assassin or the Mafioso. However, when it came to family or the ones he loved, he was dangerously protective of them. Tyson, Michael and I fell into that category. No one would have dared touch a hair on our heads. Nevertheless, when it came to our separation and then divorce, I had made it clear to him that if we were to stay together – with my sons – his criminal career had to come to a stop. This would not be easy for him. Since he had a severe language barrier, getting a regular job would be extremely difficult for him.

Being married to Taras gave us comfort and security, in the sense that we felt protected for once, rather than fearful of the man. The marriage gave me time to battle my way through the justice system while having a husband to protect me and give me emotional comfort. It also destroyed something in me. I wanted a husband who would not only protect me, love me and put me on a pedestal, but a man who respected me. Although, I think Taras respected me, as a person, he couldn't care less what I did for a living – and that bothered me – even though sometimes he appeared to be quite bothered knowing that I just came out of an appointment with a client. How could a man let his wife carry on with being a madam, even if that made the difference between keeping our children and letting them go into the hands of a monster? To this day, I have not reconciled myself with the idea that Taras had no want or desire to force me into abandoning prostitution. In fact, once I did we were no longer together. Did it end because his gravy train ended or did it end because by the end of the trial I was just so spent and things had deteriorated? To this day I do not know.

12.

There is nothing as frustrating as waiting for someone to make a decision. A decision that would affect my entire life. I waited nine months for the judge to make a decision. The trial itself was ten days in the Supreme Court of BC and media in the court room. There is murder trials that last less than half that time, then for the Supreme Court Justice to render a verdict in this case took more time than I ever expected.

It all started in 1997 and the pre-trial drudgery took over three years to be resolved. That was perhaps the most grueling time of my life.

After engaging a lawyer after firing the first one and continuing to feed him, clothe him and provide him with enough funds to build a couple of houses on the side, he managed to give me the best defense possible. His

Souled Out

name was David Halkett from Mcquarrie Hunter in Surrey, BC, Canada.

    Mike had applied for full custody of the two children in the beginning but to the Supreme Court only applied for Michael Jr. Both were still very young and far from understanding what it all meant. They only knew one thing – Michael had to spend every weekend with Mike and the rest of the time, he and Tyson were home with me and Taras. He actually spent more time with them than I ever could during that time since I was so busy trying to make money. I was the breadwinner of the family and the hours of my job were hardly what you'd call regular. At one point, I kept my brothel open 24 hours. Managing a brothel is the same as managing any business, except that your involvement becomes part of your being, part of your personality. You can never shut the office door and walk away for the night or the weekend. You become an intrinsic part of the life of others while trying desperately to divorce yourself from any thought you might have of being a sex object. It is not difficult to wash your body down, but it is impossible to erase the memories of each sex encounter. You are tattooed with the face of every man you meet. Your success depends on the regularity with which you perform. Even being a madam does not preclude you from being involved. The Calvary is a constant climb out of darkness. You want to escape but you can't. You become numb, yet addicted.

I always saw light at the end of the tunnel – I had to keep my eyes riveted on my goal, otherwise I would have lost the battle for my children and ultimately, I know, I would have destroyed myself. My children are my life. They are what I live for. If I would have lost them I would have lost my will to go on.

The waiting game didn't help, of course. However, building a case against Mike became easier as time passed but I didn't realize it at the time. He didn't have the know-how or perhaps the desire to have the children. I always thought he wanted to go through this entire procedure to exact vengeance on me. His pride was hurt, damaged to the core that yet another wife left him due to his abusive ways. For a man like Mike, that's something difficult to accept. He had been out of control when I was with him, now he was out of control because I had dared leave him. He wanted to regain his power over me, and for the whole of more than three years, he tried to do it. He failed miserably in the end, but the battle represented power to him. He had to make it last. He needed to make it last. He kept in contact with me; in a weird way he could keep tabs on me also.

Souled Out

Once he made the choice, Mike had to draw his line of attack. He wanted to demonstrate that I was an unfit mother. That was his initial mistake. He forgot, or set aside the fact that he was an unfit father or husband, for that matter. The divorce had not demonstrated the extent of his abuse or of his destructive behavior towards the children. During the trial, my Grandma Alma testified, with photographs that she had taken, of the beatings that Mike had laid on me in front of the children. My close friend, Rebecca, testified that she had seen Mike abuse and assault me as well as my own mother testified as well. Although he had retained some of the best legal advisors in the land, this bank of lawyers didn't build a case against me but managed to erect a strong case against him. Like in any battle, the warring factions need weapons and ammunitions to wage war. In this case, Mike decided to furnish his arsenal with everything he could find on me that could play against me. One of the first things he did was to hire a detective to find out how I was feeding my family and paying for my lawyer. Since our separation, Mike had no idea what I was doing but he did know that I was no longer employed by the Ministry of Transportation and Highways because he had harassed and threatened me at work so much, I had to leave.

Tania Fiolleau

However, the last time he tried I was no longer working there. I honestly believed this profession would be the last thing Mike ever would have expected. So how was I making the money then? Managing a brothel or being a madam is not something you advertise. On the contrary, it's something you do away from prying eyes. Your reputation depends on your silence. As for the money, I was earning a lot of it, not only through managing the brothel, but also through personal appearances on my website. I had built a website whereby the visitors could view some of my photos and write to me for advice. They joined with their credit cards that would be re-billed monthly so it snowballed quite fast into many fans or members. I sold modeling calendars, signed 8x10 photos and posters of myself for their walls, air fresheners for their vehicles with my photo on them and paid live appearances.

(Please note this domain or website references no longer have anything to do with me)

Souled Out

Remember, we are talking about the early days of interactive internet. This was a very rare thing, so I became quite the interest of many. I had well known porn stars working for me as well. Today, millions of websites offer the same service. However, in those days, I was one of the first. I had posted pictures of me on the website, as I said, and it worked wonders. I had scheduled times where I went online live and interacted with my thousands of fans. The clients came pouring in, asking to spend time with me. I had one man who gave me over $200,000 just to hang out with me! He was an ex-police officer, too. How crazy is that? Another flew all the way down here from San Francisco, California to spend an hour with me and he gave me $8,000 and added a $3,000 bonus for the privilege. Men were literally jumping on the plane to fly to Vancouver to spend time with their fantasy girl. If they only knew their fantasy girl was nothing more than a lost soul, deeply hurting inside, yet performing as an academy award actress in order to survive. I have had movie producers drop me over $30,000 to spend a weekend with me just to take me shopping and to the spas. I had owners of international porn companies offer me bundles of money to do a series of 10 movies putting my picture on the box and make me an overnight success and have me do appearances in Vegas, but the porn thing was far from a choice I would have ever contemplated. I had to draw the line somewhere. I once had a client buy me a brand new Jaguar sport's car cash, and another bought me a truck. I had gifts sent to me, shopping sprees and on and on, and this drove Mike wild! I never thought I was ever pretty or desirable enough to get this kind of attention. Earning this type of money was, of course, fuel for Mike's fire. It enraged him seeing me regaining my confidence and independence and having so many men fuss over me. It drove him nuts.

On the other hand, the court investigators and social services needed to ascertain that the children were well looked after. Their reports showed that the house was clean, that Michael and Tyson lived comfortably, that they were well fed and clothed, that they were going to school regularly, that their stepfather was a gentle giant who was extremely attentive to their well being, and that a nanny looked after them. That last point was a thorn in my side that could have been my downfall. "The mother is rarely home." Yet, in the end, what had become a Damocles sword hanging over my head became a powerful weapon against Mike. I repeatedly told the judge throughout the trial that the day I got custody would be the day I walked away from the business for good. Not only did Mike show antagonism toward each of the nannies he met during Michael's transfer on the weekends, but he himself, if he were to gain custody, would have had to have a nanny for the children when he went to work every day. It became a moot point during the trial.

I had no recourse, but to continue feeding my lawyer with all that I had against Mike. It amounted to years of abuse and it depicted the picture of a monster.

My lawyer mounted a defense that was hard to beat. I didn't realize at the time what he was doing, but today, I have a clear picture of what his strategy was. Mike's legal advisors wanted to demolish me in order for him to get custody. Instead of showing that he would be the better parent of the two, they tried showing that I was the "wrong" parent for them. Against that showing my lawyer put me on a pedestal and managed to demonstrate that I would be not only the better parent but also that I would be the "only" parent for these children, especially in Michael's case. What would become of the child if raised by a father who had only demonstrated a terrorizing attitude toward his mother and half brother? He already had three prior convictions of assaulting me, one of them for running over me with his truck with our son sitting beside him.... Would anyone want to see this little boy grow up into the monster his father was? No, was the answer to that question. No one would want to see a child develop under the supervision of someone who would show the boy "how much power he could have against women or everyone around him." We have enough delinquents in our society without allowing one more parent to raise a child into one. Besides which, there was Tyson to consider. His stepfather had maltreated him since he was a mere infant. He would never trust the man who had raised a hand against him and his mother so many times during his young life. This state of mind could have driven him to suicide. No one wants to have to pay the price of having made such a mistake, years down the road. Moreover, judges generally don't favor separating the children.

Both sides had many witnesses to introduce during the proceedings. The plaintiff's side took the lead. Perhaps, their star witness was the child psychologist. She tried in vain to discredit me in view of the fact that I was a prostitute. However, the undeniable fact was that the "Custody Access Reports" together with the "Child Behavior Reports" demonstrated clearly that both children were well cared for and that they had a regular, comfortable life in my home. Although I was a prostitute and a madam, I did not live the life of one. As opposed to the same reports, demonstrating that Mike's behavior was questionable not only towards the nannies that came in contact with him but the surroundings at home or his environment was not conducive to raising children. The house was clean, the fridge was full but the investigators noticed that the so-called "cleaning" or "washing" or the purchasing of food had been done when the investigator was due for a visit. When the visit was impromptu, the reports indicated clearly that his home was not welcoming to any child. If Mike were awarded custody, he, too, would be a working parent with long hours. As for analyzing the children's behavior or observing their reactions under many circumstances, the psychologist had to admit they both preferred to be home with Taras and a nanny anytime, under any circumstances. Here again, trying to discredit my ability to be a mother to these boys didn't work.

The psychologist that my lawyer engaged was a Jewish man. We had a choice between a few custody access reporters but it was Taras' idea to go with the Jewish man. We knew that Mike was (and is) an inveterate racist and an atheist. He is the begot par-excellence. He had once told me that if we had lived in the States he would have made sure to become a KKK member. He looked into it when we were together. To see a Jewish fellow on the stand passing judgment on not only his behavior, but equally describing the effect such a person would have on children was an eye opener. In appointing a Jewish psychologist to the task of evaluating the kids and asking him to pass judgment on my ability to raise my children was a stroke of genius. I am a Catholic Christian – always have been – and introducing the idea that a Jewish man could actually grant me the privilege of raising my children while knowing I was a prostitute was simply of biblical magnitude!! On top of which this psychologist was well respected around the halls of justice for having assisted in the resolution of custody battles and other cases. He had the expertise necessary to show Mike and his lawyers that life had something else to offer than beating on a wife and child. Both of Mike's lawyers could not punch holes in his testimony. If a Jewish man could openly declare in court that I seemed to be a better-suited mother for my children I was winning my case – but I didn't know it at the time.

13.

As I said, it took nine months for me to be informed

of the judge's decision, and I was at the end of my rope. If I had lost this battle, it would have meant that I slept with all those men for free, that I had dragged myself through the mud with my kids in the media and ruined my life and that of the girls – for naught. I broke down and got on my knees. I was beginning to hate God for letting me go through this. I couldn't take it anymore. I remember arguing with Grandma Alma – all the while blaspheming God – telling her that if God was real that he wouldn't have allowed me to go through this.

She rebuked me saying, "Tania, God didn't leave you. It was you who left him. He is always there and will not forsake you. You must put your complete trust in him and surrender all of your burdens to him with complete faith and he will be there. God loves you."

The next day I literally had another breakdown. Once again I was emotionally spent. I was drained, exhausted and my spirit was broken. I screamed at Him, *"God how could you let this happen to me! If you're real, give me my boys and I will quit the business and devote my life to you and make things right!"* After I surrendered it all to the Lord I slept like a baby that night which was something that hadn't happened in quite a long time. I woke up in the morning and did my usual routine; got the kids off to school and headed off to work. I stopped en-route to work for a coffee at the usual coffee shop. I ordered my coffee and grabbed the daily newspaper to see an article on the front page that stated *"Porn Industry Mom Wins Sole Custody."* I thought, "Hum, that can't be me... I am not a porn star." So I continued reading. I tell you, my knees and hands started shaking; I was barely holding it together. I panicked. I called my lawyer, David Halkett, right away to have him confirm that indeed it was me. The Lord had answered my prayers. There are no words that could describe adequately what I felt the day I receive official notification from the Supreme Court that I had been awarded sole custody of my two boys. A sense of accomplishment – a huge relief as though a concrete slab had been lifted from over my chest – I suppose, was at the forefront of my mind, yet, I was overwhelmed and a little confused. I knew I had promised the judge (and God) to quit my job, and by that I mean, quit the escort industry. Was it really true? Was I going to quit? The big question, of course, was would I be able to quit? I had to change my life. I had to divorce myself from everything and choose another path. That's easier said than done. The statistics speaks for themselves 'a lady of the night' doesn't quit, she gets out feet first.

Less than 3% of women that enter the trade get out.

Souled Out

Two thirds of their children repeat the cycle or end up in jail, and put on your seatbelt for this: *They were up to 17% higher risk to be diagnosed with PTSD (Post Traumatic Stress Disorder) than that of a POW.*

If we don't accept there is a problem, then how can we begin solving it? Obviously to solve it will take the combined work of organizations, funding, and people that really care about our children's future. The devastation that these women and men face is also a gateway to the answer. I am just here to shine the light into the darkness.

There is widespread misinformation about prostitution which is based on the media that neutralizes the harm done to the women in the industry. Brothels are completely legal in Canada. This is then spread throughout organizations that present prostitution as legitimate, that it is merely "unpleasant labor" or, in some cases, they present it as "pleasant labor" as well for the women involved.

What they need to spread is that many of these brothels are used for money laundering, human-trafficking and are run by criminal organizations. They say that it keeps the girls off the streets and safe inside. How can it be safe to be human-trafficked or working for a criminal organization? Many women start out on the streets, yet many start out in the brothels. But when they no longer can keep up with the younger competition or they develop drug habits, where do you think they eventually end up? On the streets anyway! Don't be fooled! It's just a way of sweeping the truth under the carpet so that the City can make money from licensing fees and look as though they are keeping the women safer, which they are not.

It's a LIE, people!

Prostitution is MULTITRAUMATIC whether its physical location is in clubs, brothels, hotels, motels, john's homes, motor vehicles or on the streets. It is dehumanizing to women. There are women that have said that they felt safer in street prostitution compared to legal brothels, where they were not permitted to reject any customer. Why don't we try doing some prevention here so that these women wouldn't have to *feel safer*? Others commented that on the street they could at least refuse dangerous-appearing or intoxicated customers. Yet, if we were to speak to the women that are being human trafficked in many of these brothels, (but not all) they would not say that they feel safe. If they were able to talk about their real situation, that is. Also reported there was no difference in the incidence of PTSD in the two types of prostitution, suggesting that the trauma

Souled Out

which results from prostitution is the same for ALL who are in it. It's all the same, people! I know this first hand. I worked in high-end brothels. I worked in the highest and I ran, owned and operated the best in town, and I, too, was diagnosed with PTSD (Post Traumatic Stress Disorder). Someone has to take a stand here and reveal the truth about the industry for what it really is. It is not filled with glamorous people. If you think these brothel owners and pimps are helping the women to keep them safe, you're wrong! They know the effects it has on women. Yet, they twist the truth for the simple fact that they don't want to give up their money. It's greed. *"Money is the root of all evils."* These brothel owners, organizations and pimps don't care about their girls. All they care about is the money. Just like the 'Johns' don't care about the girls. All they care about is using them for their sexual gratification.

What are we to do, as citizens of the United States, Canada and the world? There are no accidents; the harm of the sex industry outweighs the good. The institution of prostitution is carefully constructed and promoted. Those of us that are concerned with global human rights MUST ADDRESS the social invisibility, the MASSIVE denial regarding its harms. If you think that it is not affecting you or your life, then maybe you haven't noticed all the ads in magazines, newspapers, and on billboards. Maybe you haven't noticed the 'pop ups' of pornography on your computer, maybe you haven't noticed that it is considered "cool" to be a porn star. Maybe you haven't noticed our little girls dressing sexier at younger ages, maybe you haven't noticed the media throws the term "pimping" out there like it is acceptable and cool. Maybe you haven't noticed that our music is filled with themes of degrading women... And if you have, what are you going to do about it? It will continue to grow into a larger MONSTER if we continue to *accept* this social behavior. We need to stop glamorizing it. We need to get into the high schools and the colleges and all over the media. We must raise awareness and do some prevention. We need to create organizations that help re-program these women back into society. We need to stop criminalizing these women and have much stiffer penalties for the johns, recruiter, pimps & traffickers. Did you know that two-thirds of children raised by prostitutes either repeat the cycle or end up criminals? We need to protect our future generations! Did you know that 80% of prostitutes who are murdered are murdered by their johns, pimps or boyfriends?

There is one thing that I ask of all of you... Please no

longer judge these girls or men who are in the sex industry. Know that most of them are being *forced* to do it physically or mentally by the people around them, manipulating them. Please open your eyes and see that we are ALL being lied to; that most of these girls do not like what they are doing, and that it is all "acting."

Every time you say, "Those girls like what they do," pick up a "porn" magazine, watch a "porn" video, click onto that website, call that lady of the night, listen to music that degrades women (most hip hop) or go to that bachelor party or that strip club – know this: It could be your sister, your mother, your best friend's girl or your daughter and then think, is it all really worth the *thrill* of self-gratification that lasts only a couple of minutes? We are destroying lives of countless women while we do it, feeding the monster the sex industry has become. For there must be ENABLERS to create VICTIMS. Every time a man lay on top of a prostitute it takes a piece of her soul. The 'John' chooses the prostitute out of wanting. The prostitutes do not get to choose their 'John' and they do not *"want"* to be in that profession. Just remember that.

Almost all prostitutes murdered are female with approx 13% of them being between the ages of 14-16 75% are killed by johns and 12% by their pimps.

Tania Fiolleau

Street prostitution is a controversial issue, with legal, social, health and economic implications. It is also closely linked to other criminal activities. Since the act of prostitution has traditionally been considered voluntary, it has often been perceived as a victimless crime. Yet the life of a street prostitute is frequently characterized by exploitation, violence, substance abuse and disease.

Many women lead themselves to believe they're doing fine; they're okay. When you are working in this industry, you don't want to face yourself for the person you've become. You paint a caricature of yourself as a coping mechanism in order to survive, the same way I did. But once I got out of that character and I was on the outside looking in, I was slapped in the face with reality and it was traumatizing.

Most people will dehumanize the women who work in this industry. For most 'users' we are 'prostitutes' – not women. I would hate to use the old cliché of being a 'toy' in the hands of these abusers, but that's what we are. I was a 'toy', a 'prostitute' for hire, nothing else. I fulfilled their yearnings in just enough time for them to dismiss me until next time. I was at their disposal for the money! I *souled* my soul to the devil for money! Don't ever bargain with the devil. I dressed the part and I

Souled Out

acted the part for how ever long it took them to get their jollies. I didn't wait around for them to chase me out – I knew they would – and got out only looking down at the money in my hand. *I had earned the dollars and Souled myself out one more time.*

The worst part in this whole deal is that I put so many girls through the same pain that now, looking back at what I have done, I am only ashamed. My only redemption would be for me to serve God and *save the women* I could – as many as I can – from the horror of becoming less than a *human being* at the hands of these ENABLERS, these sex vultures that roam the world in quest of fulfillment of their next sexual fantasies.

14.

However, I think it is time for me to acknowledge and make it known the vicious circle into which every girl in my profession finds herself. The temptation is ever present. I can cry my eyes out about what happened to me until a river flows at my feet, but the fact remains that the need to survive surpasses the need to clean your act. To break away is harder than anyone could imagine. A drug addict needs money to satisfy his desire to get his next 'high', but when he is able to get cleaned-up, he realizes that life has much more to offer than that 'high' he sought for so long. Yet, for us, it's not a matter of getting cleaned-up or clean-up our act; it's a matter of surviving without any money to support ourselves. As I mentioned on many occasions, being drugged helps you cope with the sexual acts you perform many times with your clients. It numbs your pain. Many girls that enter the industry are not on drugs yet. The average age of entry is 12-14. They can't deal with the emotional turmoil the trade brings and they turn to drugs to numb the pain. Yet society will label them as "just another drug addict." Maybe she was forced into it and she didn't have a choice. Think about it next time you drive by a girl on the street. She is a human being. Stop de-humanizing these women. It was much harder for me as I did it straight. However, therein does not reside the problem. It resides in the fact that a madam or a prostitute lives in a vicious circle. She goes into prostitution, such as I did, because she needs money. And such as I did, my earning capacity grew thanks to my business knowledge and keeping my wits about me. Yet, others are not so lucky. I mean, they get involved with a pimp, or do not know any better than doing drugs to feel numb about the pain they endure. Therefore, it may be easy for you to say, "Why doesn't she quit the business, and just walk out?"

Souled Out

It's not an easy thing to do. If you don't perform, and bring in the cash, you might get beaten or killed in some cases. If you attempt to leave the business, *they* might hunt you down like a rat, afraid that you would reveal all of their dirty secrets to anyone willing to listen or simply want to make you pay a large amount of money to your pimp to get you out. Although the surroundings are uncomfortable, believe it or not, many of these women become comfortable in their surroundings, and they are afraid to leave for fear of not knowing where to go, where to start. Ultimately, to make that money keeps you in. Moreover, your *clients* are also afraid to find their names on some 'John's' list somewhere – they need to keep the things they do quiet. Even though they might not care who lays in bed with them on that night, they do care a lot about anyone revealing what they do – they could lose their career, or even their family and reputation. They are the 'enablers' that create the 'victims'.

Remember, I was brought up by a Catholic grandmother, who could not admit even knowing such words, but I had a father who wouldn't shy away from such cursing. I learned not to be discreet; I learned not to be lady-like. I learned to be vulgar, and I had to 'unlearn' all of it. I was like a computer that had to be completely reprogrammed. Now, every time I go somewhere, or find myself in a situation where watching my Ps and Qs is important, I *think* about what I'm going to say, before I open my mouth. As the old saying goes, 'a wise man will listen more speak less.'

Yes, I was lucky – no denying it – I was extremely lucky to be given another chance at life. For this, I thank my Lord, God. Grandma Alma has passed since but I know her prayers have been answered. I promised her on her death bed that I would do something about this plague, whatever the cost. I had to unlearn all those things that had been part of my life. I had to unlearn everything and teach myself new things. I was like a new born baby learning to walk all over again. Yes, I had to teach myself, because there's no school for ex-prostitutes. There's no one to teach you how to look at yourself, no one to make suggestions as to how you should dress, speak, or behave. You've got to do it by yourself. Nevertheless, the teachers are all around you. You need to find them and use them. Short of having a supportive family, which most of us do not have, there are people in the world who will understand what we're going through. And PLEASE, let them help you. I found that one of our greatest mistakes, however justified it may have been, is to distrust anyone who's trying to lend a hand. Such as I did for the longest time, and sometimes still do, you reject any form of assistance because you think the person has an ulterior motive. If the person is a man, he will immediately fall into the category of 'another John' and you will not take anything he says or any assistance he may offer as true or genuine, thinking and believing that he may have ulterior motives. When it comes to women, my first reaction was (and still is on many occasions) to say, "I don't make friends, I don't have friends, you should know that I don't trust anyone," meaning "watch your step, woman, I won't let you do anything to me." Maybe you'll be right some of the time, but sometimes you'll be dead wrong. Listening – without saying a word – should be another asset on your list. Listen very carefully to what people tell you (or try telling you), and don't interrupt. Even if you know it all already, just listen, and among what sounds like ramblings to you, there may be snippets of information you could use to your advantage. Listen and take in everything, and once you're home and you have a quiet moment to yourself, replay the tape of those conversations in your mind. That bit of information that you collected will be very useful someday. Put it down on your list of "helpful hints." My martial art master said to me once, "Tania, it's not the dog in the fight; it's the fight in the dog." That saying has always stuck in my mind. It doesn't matter if you are a prostitute, if you have the will and determination... You can do it!

15.

When I was finally told that I had obtained full custody of my two sons, something happened to me. It was not physical – no accident, or anything like that this time. It was something much deeper than that. My past caught up with me. I remembered, in detail, everything I did and more details and memories still creep up on me to this day. Images of being a prostitute, images of my down-trodden life, images of the torture I had accepted for the sake of my boys – they were all lining up in front of my eyes as if I had called them up one by one to my recollection. A terrible pang of guilt hit me. I felt like a failure. A shell of a woman. I felt like I lost all of my virtues. My self esteem was shot to pieces. I wanted to cleanse my entire being of those sins. I was a victim, yet I felt like a criminal. Unlike my father, I wanted to atone for my sins. I wanted to become the girl I had wanted to remain before all of this started. I was ruing the day I ever made the decision to get involved in the prostitution industry. Nevertheless, nothing is ever gained when you cry over spilled milk. If I wanted to carve a future into what was left of my life, I had to look at the possibilities – what could I do to erase the past rather than try to redress it?

The all-important thing in my life was my boys. I wanted them to know what happened to me – where I came from, how I entered prostitution and why I did the things I did. I wanted them to have some lasting memory of their mother. And that's when I decided to write this book. As I worked through this project, God's hand reached out to me again, and so did Satan's hand. It was a tug of war. On the one hand, I could accept an offer to put my name on opening and running the largest brothel in town, beside a newly erected casino and make large sums of money again, or I could leave my boyfriend and live on a disability pension for the rest of my life. As I poured my heart out and onto the pages of this book, the need to help the ones I hurt the most prevailed. Satan could take his brothel and dive down to hell with it – I wanted God as my companion and redeemer.

Tania Fiolleau

In the early months of 2010, I stored my belongings into a warehouse after I could no longer afford my rent. Since I had lost my home, I would go to the local coffee shop to gain Internet access, research this topic and type away my fingers to the bone. That was it – I was going to break away for good and do something about this. "For Good" were the two words that kept me going. For the good and the better of my life, and for ever.

I chose it to be this way. Christ bore the cross for me and I was willing to do the same for these girls at any cost. I took my car and went to a woman's shelter. After only being allowed at the shelter for 30 days, I stayed in the odd hotel then went to campsites, and eventually ended sleeping in my car. My boyfriend helped as much as he could. He paid my bills until he gave me his last red cent and mentored me along the way. During this time, I literally put him through hell. My Post Traumatic Depression (PTSD) was triggered many a time while I delved into research. I was hit with a lot of pain and reality that slapped me in the face. There were days I couldn't even continue writing for it was simply too emotionally painful.

God took Grandma Alma shortly before this time.

Souled Out

She was my only source of solace and strength. However, I had my boyfriend. At the beginning I was very distrusting towards him. It took me two years before getting comfortable with him or trusting him. I thought he had ulterior motives. I did so many things that would drive any man away but God knew what I needed and this man has the patience of a saint. He spent countless hours, days and nights talking to me, guiding me, mentoring me and supporting me in every way, at a time he was carrying heavy burdens himself. I am glad he did. It was a very rough road but one I am now glad I took. I think I have found my calling in life and I would not change any of my past or the things I went through for if I didn't I wouldn't be the woman I am today. I guess at the time I didn't understand why, if there was a God he'd allow me to go through what I did, but I understand now. *God may not be in our timing but he's always on time.* God will not allow you to go through anything that you can't handle. What I went through gave me the strength of character to reach my goal.

As soon as my son, Tyson, learned that I was alone and out of the industry, he came to join me. Today life is hard, but my heart is free and I am happier than I have ever been. I have a roof over my head once again and my son is at my side. He has entered college, and is taking criminology, criminal psychology and law. His first essay dealt with making prostitution illegal in Canada. Did you know that 74% of children raised by prostitutes are ending up in drugs or worse? There is no better reward for a mother than to see her child going to college and succeeding in life.

One last word...

YOU CAN GET OUT AND DO IT TOO!

You have to deal with it like if you were in the 12-step program – stay away from the industry all together. It must be a total separation. Take exercise classes. Find new source of friends. Go to church or any social gathering. Learn something new. Frequent women resources centers to keep busy. Be yourself and enjoy the hand of God reaching out to help you.

PART III
Life and Prostitution

16.

If I were to describe all of the relationships I had thus far in my life, there would only be a handful of words enabling me to picture the emotions, the ups and downs, the physical pain, the emotional traumas – all of the same – they hurt me deeply.

I was never happy. I was somewhat content, pleased, even delighted from time to time, but I don't think I would call any of these sentiments *happy*, or describe them as such.

Like everyone does, I suppose, I searched for happiness. I searched for joy and I sought contentment in every one of my enterprises, but I never found what I was looking for.

What am I looking for, in fact? Is it a relationship? Is it to be trusted in love? Is it to have the esteem and admiration of my peers? Or is it to have the love and cajoling from my children? To tell you the truth, I don't know anymore. I really wish I could have someone in my life that I could trust. Is this possible? I don't know. If I couldn't even trust my own parents, how could I ever trust a man when all that has ever happened was for me to being either beaten and abused or cheated on? I guess it's okay to dream. Nothing wrong with wishing for something. However, I have since discovered that you will never find happiness with someone else until you are happy with yourself first. Only then, you may choose to allow someone to come into your life and who will add happiness. Then it is a blessing. But, if they should take away your happiness causing you more stress, then my philosophy is always to find the source of it in your life, try to tackle it, and if it doesn't work... then it's simple; eliminate the source of stress.

I have battled my way through life to find peace and to find a piece of freedom amid the torment. I believe I was looking out for me; looking out for my kids – my two boys. I wanted them to be happy. Yet, I didn't know what to do. Literally, I didn't. It was not as if I could follow my mother's example – it was not an example worth even mentioning. Although I could have followed in the footsteps of Grandma Alma, and by en large I did, but my surroundings were not at all conducive to living a Christian abiding life. I basically had to raise myself since I was twelve years' old and it's not like I was really raised properly before that. I was a child raising myself. How could I know how to be a parent when I practically never had an example to follow? I did the best with what I knew, but one thing I knew for sure, was that I would go through hell or high water before I sold my kids out like my mom did. I would have been beaten for it physically and emotionally if I were to go back to a Christian life. At least that's what I thought.

Then, there were times where or when no example was necessary. My maternal instinct would take over, and I would do the right thing by the children. However, the path that I followed since I hired the lawyer is one that I perhaps should not have taken. I recognize that to be true. Yet, short of robbing a bank, I had no money that would afford me the lawyer I wanted or needed to fight my ex-husband. In the end, I believe, the boys resent what I did for them even more than I do, but they also understand. As it did me, when I was little, and I saw my mom and dad forever entangled in a bitter relationship, what occurred between Mike and me have marked the children's lives in more ways than one. As sharp as a piercing blade, Michael's remarks toward me or my behavior have a way of recalling my failures to mind. His reproaches are salient. He uses the same words as his father did but they all have the intonation of ruefulness and painful memories. He's saying, "Look what you've done, Mom. You're nothing but a whore! All you cared about was sucking cock and money instead of taking care of me! All you cared about was making money!" Of course, I cried when I heard him say this for the first time, but I then began to understand how he could feel. He wants to be like his father. He wants to follow in his footsteps and he wants to control the situation – whatever the circumstances may be – in order to avoid being hurt. I chose not to tell him how deep the abuse I suffered at the hands of his father had been. He looks up to his father so dearly, I didn't want him to be hurt any more than he had been already by putting his father down.

There is no way for anyone to change the past. There is no way to turn back the clock or to mend one's ways. There is no way I "could kiss it better." I was right and I was wrong.

I was right in wanting to free the kids from the clutches of a maniac. I would even go as far as saying that I was right in selling my shell of a body to the highest bidder so that the boys wouldn't be hurt while they were growing up. Yet, and again, I was very wrong. Very wrong to think that it would not mark me or brand them for life. In a weird sense I even became blind to what I was doing. Because I worked so much that I was around the prostitutes and 'Johns' all the time, it started to become an everyday part of life. I was becoming a product of my own environment. There was soon no separation between my attitudes in my working life and those in my personal life. I literally became a character of myself. We are not lizards that can shed their skins every year to renew their protective shell. We are not able to change our spots – once inked in, tattooed into the limbs of our actions; we will not be free of their implications. What these women fail to realize is that once you have crossed that line, you have permanently branded yourself for life. You could go and become a doctor but people won't look at you as '*Sally the doctor*', they will brand you as '*Sally the prostitute*'. This is something I have to live with for the rest of my life.

I suppose what I want now is someone beside me whom I could trust. Whose loyalty could not be swayed by ephemeral good looks or money? I want and need a man whom I could rely on and who could rely on me. As they say, trust is earned not endowed freely. It is not something you want or demand of a person or a companion; it is something you earn from the person you love. I have not yet met a man that has earned my trust completely. I either become afraid that if we have a fight they would physically assault me or they would cheat on me with another woman. To be honest, I even feared that eventually they would leave me. I will admit that I have a deep fear of abandonment. I think I

Souled Out

dreaded the pain so much; it would have felt the same as when my mother abandoned me. I know the pain all too well and I am very fearful to go through that again. It is a pain that will never leave me and that scarred me forever. I have been known to sabotage relationships with good men because when I start liking them I become so fearful of being abandoned and being wounded in the process, that I destroy it before they could dump me and hurt me. If you love anyone, trust is something you will give and impart, but it is also something you will have to merit. You won't have to compete in any great race to win a gold medal; you will simply have to be "trustworthy." Acquiring or earning trust is not a simple task either. It cannot be taken lightly and it cannot be taken for granted. Loving someone implies trusting someone, yet you could love without having an ounce of trust for that person. Conversely, someone could love you but could not trust you – what ever the reason may be.

Jealousy and trust are like the proverbial two peas in a pod. Trust should go without jealousy – yet it doesn't. If you trust someone there should not be any jealousy fraying its passage in your relationship. However, the mere fact that you are in a relationship with someone implies that you are going to be jealous of that person's time – if nothing else. You want to be with the man 100% of the time, which is a practical impossibility, but that's what you want. So many marriages have broken up for that very reason: "You don't spend enough time with me!" And that is blatant and infuriating jealousy. This jealousy would soon engender distrust if left unchecked or unbridled and would call for complete breakdown in your relationship.

I am the perfect example of such occurrences – yes, with an "s" – because there was more than one occasion when I felt the need to check on the person I loved to see where he spent all of his time when he wasn't with me.

You see, I am fiercely distrusting and that's the reason I understand men who are jealous – not that I abide by their demonstration of anger or resentment. I would even say they're perfectly entitled to be jealous IF (and that's a big IF) they're in love – truly in love – with their partner. Otherwise, it's all a sham, a demonstration of beastly control and abusive behavior, for which I have no patience, nor have I time.

The poem I wrote recently describes quite well what I feel towards the man I thought I loved and still do today.

Souled Out

"One Love"

This is about a dream I had last night
It was so real I woke up with terror and fright

We were out for walk when you turned me away
You said " You're not going to like it but I have something to say"

My face went pale and as I put my head in guard
Knowing your news would hit me quit hard

You said "I don't love you, I used you and lied."
It was my left eye that teared, but my heart that bled and cried

I said "I hate you" as I turned and ran
I looked back and yelled, "you're a shell of a man!"

You chased after me, though I drifted from sight
You became scared now, concerned that I might

You got to my house, your worst fear came true
As I stood holding the knife and yelled "how could you?"

It took that still moment to make you see
That you were blind and truly love me

Now your love was on the edge, and it wasn't an act
You told me you loved me, that you took it all back

I said it's all a lie, you don't love me,
but this kitchen knife does and it can set me free!

You started to beg, please, honey, no
But I closed my eyes and in it did go

It was so much pain I couldn't stand anymore
I dropped to my knees, then down to the floor

Tania Fiolleau

You ran to my lifeless body and crouched at my side
The pain you were now were feeling, you couldn't hide

It was all your fault, that your love took my life
It may as well have been you, holding that knife

You held my hand, and touched my face
You tried to stop the bleeding just above my waist

The last thing I said will forever be in your mind
That you killed your "One Love" and that's hard to find

You told me you loved me and you started to cry
I turned my head away, and silently died

I woke up and felt your pain so real
I just wish you were the one to see how it did feel.

This poem was called "One Love" because there is a song by Mary J. Blige & U2 called "One Love" and that was our song for we had told each other that we were each other's "one love." I wrote it after I had the dream.

Why would it be so real, if it weren't true? Why would I feel so betrayed if I didn't love you the way I do? Why does it feel so wrong to be left cold and dying once again away from trust and happiness? Perhaps I should feel guilty, but I don't – no one should for loving someone else. Perhaps I should feel angry, but I don't – love is finicky. When love hurts, there is no amount of medication or anything you can take to get rid of the unrelenting pain that a heartache gives you. I know this

Souled Out

for after that dream I found out my "One Love" was in fact cheating on me. I would prefer the worst physical pain any day over the pain that a heartache inflicts. I guess a huge part of me did die. The dream did represent something. Love is unpredictable and unwilling to allow for mistakes or error of judgment. It is just something you feel. An attraction you experience when no one is looking. A desire to be with and to "possess" the person you fantasize would be your soul mate. Yes, that's all it is – a fantasy. A fantasy you play with in your mind. A fantasy you imagine could become a reality if you behaved the way everyone thinks should bring you happiness. Isn't it just fantasy itself to think that reality could be had only if you put your mind to it? Love is forgiveness and I did forgive him. I have tried to dismiss fantasy as just that, but then it takes on another form, another disguise and becomes a wish again. A goal even. Why do I continue doing that? Maybe because my search to live a happy and peaceful life has only began. Perhaps it is my mind playing tricks on me – I don't know. Or maybe it is just the little girl in me visualizing the white wedding with all the trimmings. Being in love with one man forever and having him love me and be true to me, protecting me with his all. How wrong can one be? Or is it really wrong to yearn for someone to love you? I don't believe this is just fantasy or desire. I can't believe it is. I can only believe what is in front of my eyes. I can only believe what I want or need is simple enough for me to attain without the misery that has accompanied me to this day.

Infidelity Pain

I loved you, I trusted you
I gave you my heart
Never in an eternity
Did I think you'd tear it apart

I didn't just give you my body
I gave my love trust and soul
Then you took it for granted
Grief and despair's taking toll

Never in my life
Have I loved a man this much
I get butterflies every time
At the thought of your touch

When we made love
It was pure passion and bliss
It kills me inside to know
Another's lips you have kissed

The trauma is unbearable
I'm so numb with pain
By doing this to us
What did you think it would gain?

Was I not beautiful enough?
Were you not satisfied?
Is this why you cheated

Souled Out

And continually lied?

I loved you to the core
You were the love of my life
Now that love's turned to pain
Devastation and strife

How could something so beautiful
Cause me so much pain
Now our once happiness
Is on the heartbreak train

I don't think that I
Will ever love anyone again
I have lost the love of my life
Whom I thought was my best friend

All I ever wanted
Was for you to love me for real
I found out the hard way
It was not part of the deal

I will end this by saying
The hurt is to deep to explain
Our once love respect and trust
Now resides on Memory Lane.

I wrote this poem after I caught my love cheating on me. I honestly believe I loved this man more than I have loved anyone in my entire life. I was in bed numb with pain for days. Devastated. It killed me inside. I still love him. It is amazing how when you love so hard you can forgive after being hurt so deep. True love is agape.

17.

But, let's go back to basics. What drove you to become a prostitute? Was it a fear of being scolded or even beaten for something you did (or didn't do)? Did you just wake up one day and decided you wanted to live this life – I don't think any of us could say that. Each of us has a past. Whether we accept it, whether we can't, whether we want to forget it, or whether we refuse to let it go, there is one thing for certain, we all need to face it.

There is a mood scale®[1] developed by a scientist and psychologist that demonstrates how our brain functions and how we evolve through some of our emotions. The lowest of these emotions is apathy. Apathy is what you experience when you become indifferent to the world. You have willfully set your past aside without ever wanting to open that door again. Yet and because the world and everything in it will remind you where you have been and what you have done, you have erected a wall of ignorance around you, so that indifference is the only form of emotion you will allow yourself to feel. Apathy may protect you from being visibly hurt, but the wall will never be thick enough for you to be indifferent

---
[1] The Art of Smart Thinking, Dr. James Hardt, Ph.D.

Souled Out

forever. Something sometimes will open the floodgates and you will find yourself drowning in sadness and or depression. Sadness and depression are on the next step of the mood scale. Sadness can be an overwhelming feeling. Tell me about it! That's where I found myself so many times. It is very sad for me to think that my father only resented me or that my mother suffered from apathy during her entire life. To recall what my first husband did to me drives me to incredible sadness. As for depression, it has become the illness of our times. Anti-depressants do little to address the source of depression. All they do is send you into an artificial state of mind – one that you can't even control. Depression leads to suicide and act of uncontrollable violence. If one would only turn and look at what cause the depression in the first place, we would all be better off for it. Often times the cause resides in a deep-seated, unexpressed or suppressed rage. That rage – on the third step of the mood scale – is seldom silent, such as in Monique's case. The rage she felt against her rapist exacted itself every night onto the men she was serving. It did with me. In many instances, the rage takes on the guise of revenge. A Chinese proverb says, "The man who chooses vengeance needs to dig two graves." I have sought vengeance on quite a few occasions and all I got "in revenge" came back to bite me in the butt. Vengeance has two price tags – one for your enemy and one for you. Monique knew what I am talking about. Her price tag was much higher than that of the men who shared her bed every night. Rage or vengeance does not pay. You want to see the culprit six-feet-under, you want to see him (or her) rot in prison for the rest of his life, you want to assuage your sense of guilt by blaming everyone around you for what happened to you. "It's your fault!" you say. Yet, is it really? Where to lay blame is not the answer. The only mistake you made, perhaps, is for staying a prostitute – in a life of destruction – for so long. You don't have to blame anyone for the circumstances surrounding your life. You've made a decision, and in your rage, that decision led you down a path where fear reigned supreme. Rage is the product of fear – nothing else. Monique feared her parent's reaction; she feared the repercussions that her rape would entail. I feared my husband. I feared him most when his anger led him to maltreat my son, until my rage took over and I tried to take revenge on what he did to me. Rage also took over when I last spoke to my father. I feared him most of my life and his cruelty drove me to vengeance – to this day, I cannot but shout my anger at him. In fact, the last time we spoke, I yelled at him that I wanted him to die a slow, painful death for what he did to me. Fear is the second last of the mood scale. Fear is an all-powerful emotion that controls most of our animalistic instincts as well as our human thoughts. Fear is at the root of most of our uncontrollable reactions. Fear of the unknown is one that engenders actions of untold magnitude. "What's going to happen to me?" is the preamble question to the most violent emotions. If one cannot answer this question satisfactorily, it may drive the individual to suicide.

The last step on the mood scale is joy! You were perhaps expecting another negative emotion to top the scale. No. "Joy" is the one positive step you can reach; you need to reach before you can attain inner peace. I'm sorry if I sound like a psychologist, but this path is the one I used, and the one I recommend to anyone who wants to face their past and literally "get rid of it" for good.

Did I reach the top step? Frankly, not yet, is my answer. I've gone through all of the steps one by one, dealing with each of these emotions in turn and facing everything that happened to me with open eyes and an open mind. "But how do you reach that last step?" you ask. The answer is simple but very difficult to attain –

take my word for it. *Forgiveness* is the answer. Don't get me wrong, though, you can't just absolve anyone of his or her crime against you by walking up to the person and pronounce the words – that won't work. You're not forgiving for them. You are forgiving for you!

Once you have divested yourself of all negative emotions, whether in prayer or in any other form of contemplative situation, you will find yourself in front of the door of forgiveness. Being a Catholic at heart, I will recall the saying, "to err is human, to forgive is divine." We are no saint – that's an understatement if I ever heard one – and for any of us to forgive, truly forgive the people who have hurt us is not only difficult but practically impossible to do.

I have a friend who told me, "Forgiveness is a fabricated sentiment". She said that we try as best we can to forgive one another because we are taught it is the "right thing to do". However, if I were to discover that my boyfriend is cheating on me – again – whatever form of forgiveness I may have given him at the time of his first *human error*, will go down the steps and come out in untold rage. If I did not *forget* what he did in the first place, how could I forgive him once, twice, or even three times? Therefore, forgiveness comes at a price. Are you prepared to forgive someone who's liable to err

Souled Out

again and again? No, you're not, and I'm not! The price tag on this one is virtually too high. We are not made that way. Yes, forgiveness is divine. If you *pretend* to forgive someone in order to maintain the peace in your relationship, you're in for trouble. Remember rage? That vicious state of mind is only waiting for the next opportunity to raise its ugly head and force you to bring back the past to mind with the most virulent of results.

I'm not advocating that you should not pardon your neighbor for a little mistake now and then, no, I'm only demonstrating that without reaching the point where your past become unimportant, you will not attain the happiness we all deserve.

****

Angela was 19 years old when she was raped. "How's that possible?" you ask. Most of us think that because someone is involved in prostitution being raped doesn't apply. Think again. Angela was a freelancer. She had been successful in getting a few dates from one of the advertisers on the Internet, and on this particular occasion, she got to chatting to Gordon on line one evening.

"Hi, Gordie baby," she said. "How's my perfect man tonight?"

Gordon was hot to trot, as the old saying goes. He

had seen Angela's photos, and if this girl was anything like her pictures, he was ready to pay for her services.

"Just fine," was his terse reply. He wanted to know the "where and when" bit – and get on with it. "How about we meet at Charlie's bar for a drink – around 10 tonight?" he asked.

"Sure," Angela agreed, all smiles. This was going to be good, she thought. Another hundred for a half hour's performance would pay for that new bag she had seen in the store that afternoon.

The rendezvous was set, and Angela began preparing herself for a night she would never forget. When she arrived at the bar, she recognized Gordon instantly. He was sitting near the entrance on a barstool, sipping on what looked like a neat scotch. As he turned around when he heard Angela call his name, she smelled the alcohol on his breath. "He's already drunk," she thought, "he might be quick about it...."

Angela smoothed herself onto the stool next to him and ordered a gin and tonic, to Gordon's visible surprise. "You're not here to have a drink," he told her. "Let's get out of here. I'm not paying you to drink!"

At these words, he got up, swaying a bit on his feet, and grabbed his 'escort' by the forearm. He threw a bill on the counter with a grunt and dragged a bewildered

Souled Out

Angela out of the establishment.

"Let go of me," she yelled for all to hear. People going in or coming out of the bar just smiled and shrugged. Another 'working-woman' getting it rough, they probably thought. And rough it was going to be that night. How rough, Angela never imagined. Gordon held onto her arm firmly and led her to a neighboring building.

"Where are you taking me?" she asked breathless when the couple reached the elevators.

"To a place of fun," he replied.

When they reached the 20th floor, Gordon pushed her ahead of him and towards a door in the hallway. Angela gathered this was his apartment. In fact, it was. As he pushed her inside the door, Angela stopped, stock-still. She stared. Rising from the sofa, three other guys met her glowering eyes with a broad grin.

In the three hours that followed, Angela was gang-raped, brutalized and finally discarded on the sidewalk of the nearest hospital.

At that hour of the night, there were only nurses or ambulance attendants nearby. When they saw what happened, they took Angela in and admitted her for the night. When the intern examined her and, of course, discovered the physical damage that Angela suffered, he ordered a rape-kit.

A week later, Angela was home, nursing her wounds and re-living the emotional trauma every minute of the day. Everything in her apartment reminded her of every man she had serviced. She was a 'whore', she thought, and now she was paying the price for the bad choices she had made in life. She was the victim of a severe assault but she felt guilty. When she regained some of her strength and calmed the fury that roamed her brain, she decided to press charges against Gordon and his mates. The rape-kit would be all the proof she needed to pursue this case in court. However, what Angela could not foresee was the judge's attitude. Although Gordon had not paid for services rendered, Angela had canvassed his name on the Internet, therefore, "she had asked for it! It truly lessens the real rape cases I have seen in my court," the judge added. Of all the outrages that can be witnessed in a courtroom, that would have been a first for me. Whichever way you look at it, whether statutory or otherwise, rape is rape! What this judge was saying was that if a prostitute was raped (gang-raped in this instance) it was not *really rape* since she asked the man to render a service and, what's more, when she had the guts to present her case in court, "she lessens the *real* rape cases!"

Gordon and his friends were charged the usual $700

fine for solicitation and Angela spent a night in jail for prostitution. Not only did she have a 'wrap-sheet' now, but she would also be falling on hard-times if she tried to continue her freelancing on the Internet. There was nothing else to do but enlist her services with an agency or with a brothel.

Angela learned the basic rules of prostitution. Within a few months, that girl reached a point where she wanted to return to being a sales' clerk in one of the department stores in town. She had regained her confidence and had learned a lesson the hard way. What she also learned, however, is that men often do not "think" of doing anything wrong when engaging the services of a prostitute.

As I mentioned previously, there are *enablers who create victims.*

Let's take the majority of men. They work long hours; they are professionals and often travel away from home. Most of these men engage the services of prostitutes for one purpose only – relief. In many instances, they are tired and they don't want to face their lives at home. The children are too noisy. The wife is nagging and she does not want to have sex. Alternatively, they are single and they don't want to fuss over a woman after a hard day's work. Last are those men who have a sick urge to be in control of a woman. They are a domineering sort that cannot enact their fantasies at home. They all have one thing in common – they will use a prostitute unashamedly. They want 'relief' and they're ready to pay for it. They have no qualms about using a woman for an hour or so from time to time – much like they would go to their club and have dinner or a drink with their buddies. Women are nothing more than an object with which they can amuse themselves. There is no emotion involved – and that's the way it should be.

I told my girls often that you can't have any feelings toward your 'John', because the minute you begin to feel something for the guy, you're looking down the barrel of a whole lot of troubles. I always urged them to be as unemotional as they possibly could. If they experienced an orgasm during intercourse, they're doomed.

You see, when you've brought a man to a climax, you've done you're job. All you need to do is get out of where ever you serviced him. After that, you tick him off your list and get on to the next appointment. If you experience any kind of emotion before, during or after intercourse, that emotion will ruin you. You won't be able to perform on your next appointment and you won't be able to get the guy out of your mind. Ultimately, if you become involved with someone, you're no good to anyone.

Returning to the case I just described, New York Governor, Eliot Spitzer probably fell into the category of these men who think nothing of it when they engaged the services of a prostitute. Spitzer's case and ensuing scandal was far more reaching than anyone would have expected. As for *Kristen Davis, a competing madam that was involved in the scandal, [she] served four months of jail time on Rikers Island as a result of the scandal, and later announced a run for Spitzer's old seat in the New York gubernatorial election, 2010.*[2]

All I could say for Kristen is that although her incarceration was unwarranted, in my opinion, she found a way out of the industry at the issue of the turmoil.

If you wish to get out, you need the guts to do it. It takes more than erasing the past; it takes strength to build your future.

However, no one can build a future on the debris of life. There was a case in England that "gave notice" to the world. On December 15, 2006, a man killed five prostitutes in Ipswich's red light district. One of the questions the detectives assigned to the case asked was,

---

[2] http://en.wikipedia.org/wiki/Eliot_Spitzer_prostitution_scandal

"Why do women go into prostitution?"

Even faced with the prospect of dying at the hands of a serial killer, here is one of the answers given to the officer in charge, *"It is dangerous,"* the woman said. *"We all know it's dangerous. But it's Christmas and people need money to live."*

That's my point. Prostitutes do not 'choose' the profession for the glamour or for the money. More often than not, they are 'forced' into the street and into drugs by circumstances that are beyond their control. Mr. Harry Shapiro, a spokesperson for the charity organization, DrugScope, in England, described it very aptly. He said, *"Many of these women come from terrible backgrounds and start taking drugs to deal with that at a young age. They leave home and are very vulnerable at that stage. They often get involved with partners, who may or not act as their pimp, who may also be on drugs. Then being a street prostitute is about earning to feed that need. It is a vicious spiral that they get into."*

That "vicious spiral" as Mr. Shapiro calls it, ends up in the death of innocent women. Whether killed by a psychopath, or ending their days on earth in some back alley or run-down building, practically all street prostitutes do not, cannot return to a normal life or find a place in society. Besides, society condemns them to death before they even have a chance to live. Drugs and prostitution are intimately related. Mr. Aalders who was helping one of the prostitutes before she was murdered, stated, *"Pretty much all" of the women working the streets would have "some kind of substance misuse problem".*

He also described another victim, Anneli Aldertn, as *"someone who turned to drugs and prostitution after getting in with the "wrong crowd". It is unlikely that a woman would be able to engage in that kind of activity if she was not,"* Aalders said at the time of the investigation, adding, *"It is not drug treatment alone that would stop women working the streets".*[3]

Exactly! Using drugs is the symptom of a much deadlier disease. The emotional impact that prostitution has on the women who are in the profession is the killer. Women, and men for that matter, cannot handle the disease without taking medications against the constant resurgence of guilt.

Talking about boys, there are many stories and news worthy scoops about boys being abused during their childhood. Some of them grow up to be homosexual predators or pedophiles, some of them develop an utter

---

[3] http://news.bbc.co.uk/2/hi/uk_news/england/suffolk/6175411.stm

dislike for women or men who resembled the predominant parent – the one who did the beating or perpetrated the abuse. These young men are taught to fear men and become submissive, which is an excellent seed to plant in the mind of someone liable to become a prostitute. Male prostitutes are generally fewer in numbers than their female counterparts but they too, suffer at the hands of their 'Johns'. However, you find abused boys or closeted homosexuals in almost every community around the world. Whether visible or not, these young men live an existence of renegade and try to adapt to the conditions imposed upon them either by society or their surroundings.

Peer pressure is always a huge factor in their behavior. Being submissive, these young men submit to anyone's suggestions quite easily and follow anyone's lead without much opposition. Same as female prostitutes, they have pimps and or find themselves listed in some escort agency or other. Whether they end their lives in a hospital bed at the hands of the devastation of AIDS, or whether they succeed in getting out of the trade and find themselves a suitable partner, is really a matter of how much they are willing to give up or give in. By that, I mean whether they are willing to

Souled Out

submit to the one partner for life – literally – or how far they're willing to go in the display of sexual prowess.

This brings me to the subject of pornography and of course, porno films. Many prostitutes, male or female, go into the 'acting trade' hoping to make big money – wrong! The salaries are meager compared to what they make as escorts. Perhaps, the only advantage to having your body exposed to the porno lover is the free advertising.

I was never in porno movies, because I could not handle being watched during an intercourse, but I did take advantage of the same form of advertising. I had some excellent, tasteful photos taken and subsequently displayed on my website for quite some time. Truth being told, I never imagined I could get so many clients that way – even at a time when the Internet sex game was still in its infancy. Guys were paying a fortune to spend a few hours, a day or even a weekend with me. My first intention was to have the photos posted to advertise the sort of women the men could find in my establishment – not to have men run after me personally.

As it turned out, some men were spending fortunes to "be" with me. Talk about stroking one's ego! However, the result was the same – once they were tired of me, they would look for something (or someone) else to amuse them. At the time, I could not resist the money – the temptation of earning $200,000 just to spend a weekend with a man is quite overwhelming.

****

In the northern province of Baghlan, in Afghanistan, some former warlords hire boys between the age of 14 and 18 for sex and pleasure. The local authorities don't care one way or the other – they have other things on their minds. These boys are called "Bacha Bereesh" (a boy without beard). They are recruited by wealthy patrons to dress in women's clothes, to dance during parties and weddings and to provide their masters with the sexual pleasures their 'owners' demand of them. One of the reasons for which the recruiting of these boys is so prolific, is that women are not to be seen in public and certainly not at parties or even wedding receptions. The segregate sex practice led the men to search for pleasure elsewhere. The warlords or wealthy owners have quite of few boys in their 'harems' – the more they own, the wealthier they appear to be. *"I am not really rich, but I am just as good as the wealthy. I want as many bacha bereesh as possible, so that when I go to parties I am no worse than anybody else,"* [4] Nasro Bay explained. *"It's a good thing,"* he said. *"We have our own culture. In foreign countries, the women dance. We have our own dances which don't exist anywhere else in the world."*

These boys grow up to become "Bacha Bazi" (Play boy). This is a tradition that dates back to ancient times, and although condemned by Muslim clerics and by human rights activists, it is still common practice in northern Afghanistan. The head of the northern branch of the Afghan Independent Human Rights Commission, Mohammad Zaher Zafari, condemns the government's inability to take action. *"Unfortunately I have to say that this type of dancing, sexual abuse and even the sale of boys has been going on for years,"* he said. *"It is a despicable culture. The boys involved are usually poor, underage or orphans and they are forced into it by their economic circumstances."*[5]

I am sure you have notice the common thread here. Whether we are talking about an escort from a renown agency in New York or a 'Play Boy' from northern Afghanistan, both are "forced into [the trade] by their economic circumstances."

---

[4]http://www.digitaljournal.com/article/246409/Boys_in_Afghanistan_Sold_Into_Prostitution_Sexual_Slavery

[5]http://www.digitaljournal.com/article/246409/Boys_in_Afghanistan_Sold_Into_Prostitution_Sexual_Slavery

Tania Fiolleau

"*I was dancing last night,*" one exhausted-looking fourteen-year-old boy said when his owner forced him to speak. "*I have been doing this for the past year. I have no choice - I'm poor. My father is dead, and this is the only source of income for me and my family. I try to dance well, especially at huge parties. The men throw money at me, and then I gather it up. Sometimes they take me to the market and buy me nice clothes.*"

When we complain about our circumstances, how the government does too little too late for the prostitutes of our western world, I turn my mind to the 14 year-old dancing for his owner in some back country. Then I think of my sons. We are not well off, by any means, but at least Tyson is with me. He is 19 years old now, and I thank God at every opportunity for enabling me to still take him in my arms. Can you even imagine what prostitution and the condoning of the practice does to young women and men growing up in such an environment?

This brings me back to the enablers – these men who think nothing of taking a woman to bed for their eight-second pleasure. These eight seconds turn into a lifetime of turmoil for the woman who makes prostitution a means of earning her next dollar. When you look into the history of prostitution you find

Souled Out

thousands of cases where men 'enabled' women to be a prostitute. *Prostitution was a part of daily life in ancient Greece. In the more important cities, and particularly the many ports, it employed a significant proportion of the population and represented one of the top levels of economic activity. It was far from being clandestine; cities did not condemn brothels, and they existed in plain view.*[6]

Whether you are willing and even able to get out of the industry, such as I was, you cannot forget and you cannot accept what happened to you easily.

****

In most communities of this world, women are not born to be prostitutes but for many it is their destiny. Yet there are many who are "driven" to become the prostitutes that you meet on the street or in an alley of some dark neighborhood. Others are qualified as "escorts" or "companions" or "call girls" for the night or even for just an hour. Whether we call them "whores," "prostitutes," "hookers," "call girls" or "escorts," they are women who have less than a three percent chance of ever getting out. These are scary statistics and I will tell you why...

---

[6] http://en.wikipedia.org/wiki/Prostitution_in_ancient_Greece

Tania Fiolleau

Prostituted women are 60-120 times more likely to be murdered than the public. The statistics will classify them as "drug addicts," "one more dying from aids" or "one more hooker murdered."

Statistics on Violence against Woman[7]

- Before a police report is made, a woman has already been assaulted as many as 35 times!
- Assault of woman happens in all education and income brackets and in all religious and ethnic groups.
- Children who witness abuse and violence are as traumatized as much as they would be if they had suffered the abuse themselves. *This is something I know from experience first hand.*
- A woman killed in BC is more likely to have been killed by her partner than by anyone else, and she is more likely to be injured by her partner than in a car accident.
- Women are 13 times more likely to be abused in their own homes than by a stranger on the street. *I unfortunately fell into that category.*

---

[7] http://www42.statcan.ca/smr08/2006/smr08_012_2006-eng.htm

- Children from abusive homes are at a greater risk of abusing or being abused. *I unfortunately fell into that category.*
- Violence affects all family members whether they show the effects or not.
- Four out of five victims of sexual assaults reported to police say they were attacked by someone they know.
- 1 out of every 2 women in Canada has been physically or sexually assaulted at least once (from the age of 16). This figure represents 51% of 10 million women. *I unfortunately fell into that category.*
- 1 in 3 woman experience physical assault, from threats of assault to attacks causing serious injury. *I unfortunately fell into that category.*
- Children witness violence in 4 out if 10 marriages where violence is reported. *I fell into this category.*
- 45% of victims know their attackers. *I did.*
- 29% of women have experienced violence at the hands of a present or former partner. *I did.*
- 15% of woman experience violence by the men they still live with.

- 63% of woman attacked by their male partner are assaulted more than once; 32% are assaulted more than 10 times. *I was.*
- Only 14% of violent incidents against woman are reported to the police.

When I was in the trade, I managed two brothels and had several hundred women work for me over the years. When I took over the second one, it was considered the "grandfather of all brothels," but its revenue was the lowest of all those that were still in business at the time. I turned the deficit into profit in less than a year. Why? Because I thought I cared and I needed the money. I thought I cared for *my girls*. I wanted them to have the best. I wanted them to feel comfortable, not forced into anything they could not or would not do. Mind you, I was ruthless and dispassionate about the whole thing. I had learned to divorce my business mind from my conscience or the compassion I felt for the girls in order to survive.

Yes, for me it was a business, and for them it was steady employment. Both business and employment came at a cost. They were losing their youth, pride, self-esteem, but most importantly, their self-worth, and virtues. I was losing my mind to grief, self-loathing and a guilty conscience, knowing that I was contributing to destroying their lives. It was killing me inside but the thought of losing my babies made me do the unthinkable.

What can we do about it, you ask. Not only can we help them get out, but we can raise awareness and do some prevention! Knowing the industry such as I do, I want to see the ninety-seven percent of no-return-to-normal life decrease. I want to help these girls get out of the vicious circle before we find them dead in some dark alleys or become another statistic in the wrong column. The ads that these women see such as the one that lured me into the industry are not what they are made out to be. I, too, am guilty of placing these ads and luring women in – innocent women – who will soon become victims, however, I didn't realize I was guilty until years later when I saw the damage it did to me and the girls. Ads, such as, "Earn up to $1500 daily. Female owned and operated..., safe fun, friendly working environment," bla, bla, bla, are all lies!

Talking to them should be the first step. It would be a ladder to climb out of the pit of despair. Of course, the world wasn't made in one day, and neither would this project. Like one of my friends said, "To make all your secret dreams come true, just take that first step, then follow through." If I only could save one girl from endless torment, I would be satisfied to have taken at least one step in the right direction.

After seeing the damage I had done, I decided to take a stand for these women and do whatever it took to write this book, research the topic, raise awareness, etc. The majority of women I talked to stated that they were still doing it because they didn't know what else to do. They had no resources to exit the trade. I was overwhelmed with incredible guilt and sadness; I could no longer stand the idea of taking money from a girl that had literally sold a piece of her soul every time she 'turned a trick'.

I came in contact with more and more women and repeatedly came across the same thing. Many of them had aged immensely and developed drug habits in a very short time. I started researching statistics and was amazed when I learned things such as less than 3% of women that enter the trade get out. I know the pain I felt and had suffered all too well. There and then, I

Souled Out

made the decision to take a stand for these women and do something about their plight.

18.

In response to the question "what is prostitution?" I would like to define the word according to Webster's Dictionary. **Prostitution**: the practice of engaging in relatively indiscriminate sexual activity, in general with individuals other than a spouse or friend, in exchange for immediate payment in money or OTHER valuables.

The commercial sex business consists of these "types" of selling:

Street prostitution, massage brothels, escort services, outcall services, strip clubs, lap dancing, phone sex, adult and child pornography, child prostitution, video and internet pornography, trafficking, and prostitution tourism.

Now that we have defined prostitution, what then, is "pimping?" According to the same dictionary, a "pimp" is a man who solicits clients for a prostitute, to make use of, often dishonorably, for one's own gain or benefit. A pimp is the man or woman, who procures the prostitute, promotes, *sells* her, and profits from the prostitution.

By definition, pimps are not only the men on the street, pimps are also strip club owners, bar owners, disc jockeys, taxi drivers, concierges, motel managers, etc. All these venues will profit in some way or another, if they engage in promotion of the woman or man.

What then, is a "trick" or a "john?"

John: a prostitute's client.

I used to use the term "trick" or "date." The word trick comes from customers practices of tricking women into doing more than they pay for; the word date suggests that prostitution is a normal part of male-female relationships. It's all a lie – just to make it sound more "acceptable."

Now you are a little more educated as to what the world of the sex industry is. It is a sick world, full of broken dreams and empty promises, battered, shattered, sexually abused women, men and children. And it needs to stop! The sex industry is destroying our families, it is causing alarming divorce rates, teen pregnancies, STDs-AIDS, drug usage, not to mention altered views of what sex really means!

Buckle your seatbelts, below are the stats on prostitution in Canada:

(The following are statistics that I have gathered from various places such as Census, Statistics Canada, websites advocating against prostitution, etc. No one really knows the "exact" statistics because in my

Souled Out

opinion this seems to get swept under the carpet and not really something in which society has been educated. In Census and Statistics Canada their stats were outdated as far back as 1995 – what does that tell you?)

AGES:
    Average age of entry: 14-16 yrs.
    Average years in prostitution: 21
    Percent younger than age 18 at entry: 44%

VIOLENCE IN PROSTITUTION

Traumatized individuals tend to minimize or deny their experiences, especially when they are in the midst of ongoing trauma, such as war combat or prostitution. This leads to a decreased rate of reporting violent crimes. Please understand that many of these girls are afraid of their pimps, and if they told everything that is actually going on behind closed doors, they'd fear violent retaliation from the pimp or death. Many of these girls are in an emotional relationship with these pimps where they are completely brainwashed and too insecure or afraid to leave them. Many get so used to the money they are afraid to step back into the real world.

    Threatened with a weapon: 78%

Physically assaulted: 82%

Raped: 82%

Many women in this business are confused with the definition of rape. If rape is as unwanted sex act or coerced, then the statistic would be a much higher percentage. Some women in prostitution assume there is no difference between prostitution and rape, and they only call it rape if they were not paid, regardless of the violence of the act – asking them is like asking someone in a combat zone if they are under fire. A significant percentage of women currently prostituting deny rape and other violence because it would be too stressful to acknowledge the extreme danger posed by johns and pimps!

Raped more than five times: 73%

Current or past homelessness: 84%

As a child, was hit or beaten by a caregiver until injured or bruised: 49%

Sexually abused as a child: 65-95%

PROSTITUTION AND PORNOGRAPHY

Upset by an attempt to make them do what had been seen in pornography: 32%

Pornography made of her in prostitution: 49%

DRUGS AND ALCOHOL USAGE

Drugs: 78%

Alcohol: 36%

WHEN ASKED, "WHAT DO YOU NEED?" TO PROSTITUTES

Would you leave prostitution: 87%

Need home or safe place: 78%

Need job training: 73%

Need health care: 58%

Need peer support: 60%

Need legal assistance: 42%

Need alcohol and drug treatment: 77%

Self-defense training: 49%

Need Physical protection from pimp: 28%

Note: most women will not say that they need protection, because they are mentally still "in love" and in denial that the pimp will come and look for them. I believe the percentage is as high as 80%, from experience of knowing what the pimps are capable of.

Need individual counseling: 58%

Quick to note from experience with friends, and myself most women are in denial of the fact that they need counseling, and avoid it by doing drugs and drinking. So, I would comment this is a much higher rate than reported, more like 85%. Most would have already developed Post Traumatic Stress Disorder the first time they were sexually violated.

Post Traumatic Stress Disorder: definition – psychological consequences of exposure to, or confrontation with, stressful experiences that the person experiences as highly traumatic. The experience must involve actual or threatened death, serious physical injury, or a threat to physical and/or psychological integrity.

I was diagnosed with Post Traumatic Stress Disorder after exiting the industry.

People most likely to develop PTSD: PROSTITUTES, PORN STARS, rape victims, battered women, childhood sexual abuse, a person experiencing psychological or physical torture, witnessing the death of a loved one, natural catastrophes, bad trip on drugs, and WAR or COMBAT EXPOSURE .

PTSD has been called "shell shock," "battle fatigue," "accident neurosis," and "post rape syndrome." It has been often misunderstood or misdiagnosed, even though the disorder has very specific symptoms that form a definite psychological syndrome. In some cases the symptoms of PTSD disappear with time, but in most cases they will persist for many years, and cause severe depression, nightmares, insomnia, night terrors, anxiety attacks, flash backs, emotional detachment or numbing of feelings, hyper-sensitivity to loud noises, altered state of mind. Many need professional help to recover successfully from the psychological damage that can result from experiencing, witnessing, or participating in an overwhelmingly traumatic event.

I still suffer from many of these things to this day.

These girls experience rape, pimping (psychological torture), physical abuse, medical conditions and diseases that threaten death, addictive behaviors such as drug usage, suicide attempts, bulimia, anorexia, poor self image issues, anxiety attacks, and mood swings, to mention a few.

These girls need OUR help to recover—they need pastors, mentors, family, and friends all to support them as they "walk out" their pain.

Diagnosis of PTSD in Canada due to prostitution: 76%

Diagnosis of PTSD for combat war veterans: 69%.

This is very interesting to note—these women in the sex industry are just as traumatized if not more than someone in combat on the front lines! However, society chooses to sweep it under the carpet.

If no one condemned brothels in Athens in the antiquities, no one is doing anything about it – or very little – in North America today either.

The following excerpts from various sources will show you what we're dealing with.

(I give my sincere thanks to all of the journalists and writers or prime movers who have taken the time to put the facts down for all of us to acknowledge.)

POLICY AND LAW

Women prostitution

In April 1998, Sudbury Regional Police launched the DISC (deter, identify, sex trade, consumers) program. The program targets the anonymity of the johns who buy sex from women in prostitution. The operation has focused on Elgin and Durham streets, and the Medina Lane area, after regular business hours. People who speak to, stand with, or continually drive by the prostitutes can be stopped, watched or be asked to provide identification by the police. In the first five months, police charged 16 men and seven women with prostitution-related offences through the DISC program.

Souled Out

Two of the cases involved prostitutes younger than 16 years of age.[8]

Aggravated pimping, in cases involving violence and commercial exploitation of youth, mandates a minimum sentence of five years imprisonment.[9]

Escort Prostitution

In Toronto, Canada, prostitution is not illegal, but communicating or discussing sex for cash is one of four Criminal Code offenses governing the escort agency trade. However that law was just changed in Ottawa in September 2010 when Justice Tracy Hamill handed down her decision

An Ontario court has thrown out key provisions of Canada's anti-prostitution laws in response to a constitutional challenge by a Toronto dominatrix and two prostitutes in 2009.

Ontario's Superior Court of Justice ruled [recently that] the Criminal Code provisions relating to prostitution contribute to the danger faced by sex-trade workers.

---

[8] Staff writer, "Prostitution on the rise in Sudbury, group says," *Sudbury Star*, 14 August 1998
[9] "Canada's Paper for EU Conference on Trafficking in Women for Sexual Exploitation" 10-11 June 1996

P.O.V

Canada's prostitution laws: Did the judge make the right call?[10]

In her ruling, Justice Susan Himel said it now falls to Parliament to "fashion corrective action."

"It is my view that in the meantime these unconstitutional provisions should be of no force and effect, particularly given the seriousness of the charter violations," Himel wrote.

"However, I also recognize that a consequence of this decision may be that unlicensed brothels may be operated, and in a way that may not be in the public interest."

The judge suspended the effect of the decision for 30 days. It does not affect provisions dealing with people under 18.

Federal Justice Minister Rob Nicholson and Rona Ambrose, minister for the status of women, both said the government is concerned about the decision and "is seriously considering an appeal."

Dominatrix Terri-Jean Bedford, Valerie Scott and Amy Lebovitch had argued that prohibitions on keeping a common bawdy house, communicating for the purposes of prostitution and living on the avails of the

---

[10] http://www.cbc.ca/canada/story/2010/09/29/mcguinty-prostitution.html

trade force them from the safety of their homes to face violence on the streets.

The women asked the court to declare legal restrictions on their activities a violation of charter rights of security of the person and freedom of expression.

The women and their lawyer, Alan Young, held a news conference Tuesday afternoon and expressed elation.

"It's like emancipation day for sex-trade workers," said Bedford, adding the ball is now in Prime Minister Stephen Harper's court. "The federal government must now take a stand and clarify what is legal and not legal between consenting adults in private."

'This decision means that sex workers can now pick up the phone and call the police and report a bad client.'— *Valerie Scott*

Scott called it an amazing victory, saying the decision lessens the risk of violence for sex workers.

"We don't have to worry about being raped and robbed and murdered," she said. "This decision means that sex workers can now pick up the phone, and call the police and report a bad client. This means that we no longer have to be afraid, that we can work with the appropriate authorities."

Moreover, sex workers can set up guilds and associations, health standards, workers' compensation programs, as well as pay income tax. "We want to be good citizens and it's time, now we finally can," said Scott.

Young handled the case mostly free with the help of 20 of his law students. They were up against nearly a dozen government lawyers.

"Personally, I am overjoyed because this is a great David and Goliath story. Sex-trade workers are disenfranchised and disempowered, and no one has listened to them for 30, 40 years," Young said.

Ontario AG considers appeal

The case does not solve the problems related to prostitution, he said.

"That's for your government to take care. Courts just clean up bad laws."

"So what's happened is that there's still going to be many people on the streets and many survival sex workers who are motivated by drugs and sometimes exploited by very bad men. That's not going to change," Young added.

Souled Out

"Here's what changed. Women who have the ability, the wherewithal and the resources and the good judgment to know that moving indoors will protect them now have that legal option. They do not have to weigh their safety versus compliance with the law."

A spokesman for Ontario's attorney general said the office will be reviewing the decision carefully and will consult federal colleagues regarding a potential appeal.

"Ontario intervened and argued that the prostitution provisions of the Criminal Code are constitutional and valid and designed to prevent individuals, and particularly young people, from being drawn into prostitution, to protect our communities from the negative impacts of street prostitution and to ensure that those who control, coerce or abuse prostitutes are held accountable for their actions," said the statement from the Ontario attorney general's office.

The government had argued that striking down the provisions without enacting something else in their place would "pose a danger to the public."

'Shocking and horrific'

Some conservative groups such as REAL Women of Canada, which had intervener status in the case, argued that decriminalizing prostitution may make

Canada a haven for human trafficking and that prostitution is harmful to the women involved in it.

While prostitution is technically legal, virtually every activity associated with it is not. The Criminal Code prohibits communication for the purpose of prostitution. It also prohibits keeping a common bawdy house for the purpose of prostitution.

Those laws enacted in 1985 were an attempt to deal with the public nuisance created by streetwalkers. They failed to recognize the alternative — allowing women to work more safely indoors — was prohibited.

The ban on bawdy houses is an indictable offence that carries stiffer sanctions, including jail time and potential forfeiture of a woman's home, while the ban on communication for prostitution purposes is usually a summary offence that at most leads to fines.

The provisions prevent sex-trade workers from properly screening clients, hiring security or working in the comfort and safety of their own homes or brothels, Young said.

Young cited statistics behind the "shocking and horrific" stories of women who work the streets, along with research that was not available when the Supreme Court of Canada upheld the communication ban in 1990.

I happen to blatantly disagree with her decision. I feel that she is not fixing the problem at all. From my experience as a madam, I have witnessed over the years that many of the women who start off working in brothels, eventually end up on the street. They can no longer be responsible and hold down their shifts in a brothel. Whereas on the streets they can come and go as they please. Many eventually end up on the street when they either can't keep up with the competition or they have developed drug habits. This judge hammering down this decision has basically made the less than 3% of no return go down to virtually nil. She is basically fostering the growth of the industry.

It is my strong opinion that what MUST be done is to create organizations that not only help rehabilitate these women back into society and get them out of the sex trade all together, but we also need to create organizations that will get into high schools, colleges, etc. to do some serious prevention work. Considering there are proven statistics that show that up to 2/3 of prostitutes' offspring will end up repeating the cycle or end up career criminals. We need to protect our future generations. By legalizing it, these statistics will only climb much higher.

In The Greater Toronto Area, *Now Magazine* was charged in 1990 with 14 counts of "communicating" for the purpose of prostitution because of its escort agency ads in the classified section. The charges were dropped in what one crown prosecutor called a "political decision" and the advertising floodgates were opened.[11]

The city of Vancouver B.C collects approximately $3,500 from each of the 100 'body rub parlors' and escort agencies.[12]

In the "Shame the johns" Campaign, Vancouver, British Columbia police plan to release the names of men suspected of trying to buy women in prostitution.[13]

Human trafficking for prostitution

1,000 employment authorizations for foreign exotic dancers are issued every year.[14]

There is no section specifically on trafficking in women in the Criminal Code of Canada, and

---

[11] Nick Pron "Dating Services Bring Boom Times to Prostitution" *Toronto Star* (1997)

[12] Jon Lowman, Greg Middleton, "Law Blamed for Hooker Murders," *The Province*

[14] "Canada's Paper for EU Conference on Trafficking in Women for Sexual Exploitation" 10-11 June 1996

prostitution is not illegal in this country, therefore Immigration Officers cannot refuse entry or issue a removal order to individuals solely on the grounds that they engage in prostitution.

Recruitment of exotic dancers into Canada is legal, and may be linked to the issues of trafficking and sexual exploitation. Women who enter Canada to work as exotic dancers are vulnerable to sexual and economic exploitation, deprivation of freedom, and can be coerced into criminal activities, whether they have entered legally or illegally. There have been many reports of extortion, coercion, rape and prostitution involving foreign exotic dancers, strip club managers and patrons. Foreign exotic dancers tend to be recruited in their country of residence by "talent agencies." The talent agency pays all up-front costs associated with travel and initial accommodations. The loan becomes a form of debt-bondage. Many of these women do not speak French or English and are unfamiliar with the legal protections available to them under Canadian law. Women are regularly transported back and forth across the Canadian-US border for the purpose of prostitution.

Tania Fiolleau

Canadian law enforcement has long been aware of this.[15]

750 criminal charges were filed against traffickers in one case of bringing women from Southeast Asia to Toronto for prostitution.[16]

Child Pornography

A new law in Canada, the Protection of Children Involved in Prostitution Act, increased the fines for both pimps and male buyers to $25,000 from $2,000. Pimps and male buyers are warning their peers of the new law, via the Internet.[17]

The Protection of Children Involved in Prostitution Act in Canada will provide the legal means to remove children in prostitution from the streets and put them back into their homes or into protective custody. It also calls for higher fines on anyone encouraging children into prostitution.[18]

I feel strongly that we need to have far way stiffer penalties for the johns, recruiters and pimps and give

---

[15] "Canada's Paper for EU Conference on Trafficking in Women for Sexual Exploitation" 10-11 June 1996

[16] Bill Wallace & Benjamin Pimental, "San Jose Women Held After Raid in Sex Slave Case," *San Francisco Chronicle*, 13 September 1997

[17] Bart Johnson, "Creeps Scared Off Internet Warns Pimps, Johns That Sex With Underage Hookers In Alberta is Child Abuse," *Edmonton Sun*, 1 May 1998

[18] Rob Flanagan, "Bartolucci's bill passes second reading," *Sudbury Star*, 29 May 1998

them lengthy jail sentences in order to deter them from recruiting, exploiting and extorting these women. This will lower the demand, in turn lowering the supply. This would definitely be a good start in the right direction.

In Alberta the Child Welfare Act was amended to classify the hiring of prostitutes under 18 as child abuse. Convicted buyers face fines up to $2,000 or six months in jail. In 1997, new federal legislation made it an offense to seek the sexual services of a person believed to be less than 18. The new law also sets a minimum five-year federal prison sentence - with a 14-year maximum - for pimps who coerce juveniles into prostitution through violence or intimidation.[19] *In my opinion this is too lenient. This could be your child!!*

A person convicted of living off the avails of child prostitution was judged by a British Columbia government screening program as being "no risk," and allowed to keep a job that involves contact with children.[20]

Canada discarded the principle of double jeopardy, so a person can be prosecuted for extra-territorial crimes of sex exploitation both in the country where the crime is committed and in Canada.[21]

---

[19] "Alberta Justice Minister Wants Jail for Johns," *Associated Press*, 1997
[20] Stewart Bell, *Vancouver Sun*, October 1997
[21] "Child sexploitation within law's reach," *The Nation*, 2 July 1997

Tania Fiolleau

In 1997, Canada made it illegal for citizens to have sex with children in foreign countries. *This should be illegal in all counties, people. How can any country legalize having sex with children?*

Each year, thousands of western tourists travel to impoverished Third World countries and Eastern Europe to buy children in prostitution.[22]

This is simply demonic perversion! Did you know that many of the missing children that are on milk cartons, posters etc were kidnapped and sold into sex slavery?

According to Canadian law, men who buy a child in prostitution in a foreign country face up to 10 years in prison, while in Canada, they face 5 years in prison.[23]

Canadian customs agents and police have special powers to prosecute child pornography peddlers and child-sex tourists under Bill C-27, passed in 1997.[24]

Cases

A family run prostitution network in Canada made more than $1 million in two years by prostituting foreign women. A man, his son, his wife, their daughter and daughter-in-law all recruited females who

---

[22] Ian Bailey, "Ex-prostitute offers reality check on tactic against sex tourism," *CP*, 12 March 1998

[23] Police, Kimberly Daum, "Sexually Exploited Children in Canada: The Law is Not on Their Side," *Opinion/Essays*, 17 October 1996

[24] Tom Godfrey, "Sex tourists targeted," *Toronto Sun*, 11 September 1998

Souled Out

participated in the overall operation. Many of the 20 prostitutes – aged 23 to 39 – were related to the operators by marriage or blood, Murarotto said. They worked out of apartments and each turned over at least $15,000 a year to the operators.[25]

Xuong Han Luong faces charges of owning a brothel in Toronto, Canada, and living off the avails of prostitution. He held at least five Thai women in the brothel, forcing them into prostitution. Although the brothel was raided in 1996, police believe the same group reopened it.[26]

Adam Jermaine Ingram, 20, and Kevin Roy Woods, 18 are accused of paying $3,000 to buy a 13-year-old girl from a man in Vancouver, Canada, abducting her and her friend and raping them while on route to San Diego. Their actions violate, among other laws, the 1948 White Slave Traffic Act, prohibiting the transport of minors across state lines with the intent of engaging in criminal activity.[27]

11 women, aged 18-25, from the former Soviet Union, were forced to become exotic dancers in a strip club. The women were recruited from the former Soviet

---

[25] George Christopoulos, "Family Ran Prostitution Ring," *Toronto Sun*, 16 May 1998

[26] Rob Lamberti, "Cops Raid Den of Thai Sex 'Salves' 2 Men Arrested For Running Bawdy House," *Toronto Sun*, 10 May 1998

[27] "Teen Girls Abducted," *The Province*, 21 December 1997

Union with the promise that they would become highly paid models in Canada. They entered Canada illegally, and the traffickers took their passports and other identification and held them in Toronto. The women went to the police in April 1991. Two men were charged and fined $1000 and $2000.[28]

This is no incentive to make them not do the same thing again.

One Asian woman who was trafficked into Canada 10 years ago at the age of 17, reports that agents traffic at least 30 Thai women into Canada per trip, and that there are at least 3 Thai agents in Toronto alone.

I'm sure by now these numbers have quadrupled.

Prostituted women are 60-120 times more likely to be murdered than the general public. The murder of prostituted women in Canada continues to rise. From 1991-1995 63 prostituted women were murdered in Canada, 26 of which in British Columbia. More than half of the cases remain unsolved. Six to eight others were murdered in 1996 and 1997 in B.C.[29]

The numbers have greatly risen since then and will now rise even faster with prostitution now being legal.

---

[28] "Canada's Paper for EU Conference on Trafficking in Women for Sexual Exploitation" 10-11 June 1996

[29] Dr. John Lowman criminologist, Paul Dillon, "Life On The Streets in Dangerous," *Surrey Leader*, 17 May 1998

Souled Out

Statistics on the murders of prostitutes in the Vancouver area: 1960-1977 1; 1978-1980 4; 1981-1985 12; and 1986-1995 60.[30]

I have no current statistics but I am sure they are considerably higher. And since there seems to be a lack of updated statistics in the recent census and in Statistics Canada, one could conclude that society has swept the negative aspects of the sex trade under the carpet.

Within 5 days, two prostituted women were murdered in Vancouver. Many of the murders against prostituted women go unsolved, such as 19 unsolved murders between 1988 and 1994.[31]

Women and children in street prostitution comprise 1/3 of the 1,500 people in the sex industry in Montreal.[32]

I had a girl that once worked for me. She decided to start working off Craig's List out of her home. She had her babysitter take her 3 children across the street to the park while she was with her john. The babysitter came back to find her murdered. Her pimp is a suspect in her murder.

---

[30] Jon Lowman, Greg Middleton, "Law Blamed for Hooker Murders," *The Province*
[31] Peter Montague, RCMP media liaison statistics, Dawn Brett, "Angry mourners demand action," *Vancouver Sun*, 14 June 1997
[32] Police estimates. "Prostitutes protest police sweep" *Montreal Gazette,* 23 June 1998

Tania Fiolleau

The Coalition for the Rights of Sex Workers, a lobby group representing about 5,000 prostituted persons, escorts, strippers and phone-sex operators in Montreal, held a small demonstration at the riding office of Quebec Employment Minister Louise Harel. They were demanding the same rights as other workers in the province. Coalition spokeswoman Marie-Claude Charlebois said working conditions in the sex trade are deplorable. "We're sick of having no say when it comes to wages, working hours or working environment," she said. Women engaged in prostitution on the streets often work in dangerous, isolated areas that offer no protection against violence from clients, pimps and even police, Charlebois said.[33]

Like I said, if we imposed stiffer penalties to the pimps, recruiters and johns, it would prevent these women from working on the streets. We don't need to legalize prostitution and bring them inside to do so. Many women inside are pimped and forced into working anyway. Legalizing the problem does not solve it.

There are far more than 15,000 prostitutes in the Greater Toronto Area, and more than 6,000 women are in the escort trade. One hour costs a minimum of $150, with half usually going to the agency. Women escorts

---

[33] "Sex Workers seek rights," *Ottawa Sun*, 6 September 1998

are "busiest" during corporate conventions held in the area. A recent trend is for women to operate as "independents" that book their own dates and run ads on the Internet.[34]

Of prostitutes known to be on the streets of Sudbury, Canada half are under 15 years old and some are as young as 11.[35]

70 to 80% of those involved in the Canadian sex industry began as children. And 80 to 95% are fleeing sexual abuse that usually began at home.[36]

In Canada, the escort service has become a booming underground economy, at an estimated $1/2 billion annually.

I am sure it's actually much higher than this.

The number of agencies has increased from just a few, a decade ago, to more than 150 in the Greater Toronto Area alone.

This does not include the illegal brothels run out of apartments, etc.

Men run most of the larger agencies in the Greater Toronto Area, the biggest of which employs about 100

---

[34] Detective Mark Marple of Peel Region Police Nick Pron, "Dating Services Bring Boom Times to Prostitution," *Toronto Star*, 1997

[35] Police, Wayne Chamberlain, "Half of Sudbury Prostitutes Under 15 Years Old, Police Say: Streetwalkers a growing problem in Nickel City," *The Sudbury Star*, 13 April 1998

[36] Kimberly Daum, "Sexually Exploited Children in Canada: The Law is Not on Their Side," *Opinion/Essays*, 17 October 1996

women. Other small agencies have between 2 and 6 women.[37]

I believe that many of these are run by organized crime as well.

Setting records is part of the competition among escort agencies. 12 men reportedly bought one woman in one night. One agency auctioned a woman as a virgin. The "bidding war" resulted in a record hour fee of $800.[38]

This was also done by Dennis Hoff the owner of the Bunny Ranch in Nevada who auctioned off a virgin for more than 1 million dollars.

200-300 juveniles in prostitution in Vancouver are routinely arrested on prostitution-related charges.[39]

Hundreds of children under 17 years old are being exploited in the sex industry in Vancouver, Canada. Middle-aged male buyers are increasingly seeking girls as young as 11. The police are not trusted by the children, who have targeted them for arrests rather than the perpetrators.[40]

---

[37] Toronto Star investigation, Nick Pron, "Dating Services Bring Boom Times to Prostitution," *Toronto Star*, 1997
[38] Police files, Nick Pron "Dating Services Bring Boom Times to Prostitution" *Toronto Star* (1997)
[39] Youth workers, Kimberly Daum, "Sexually Exploited Children in Canada: The Law is Not on Their Side," *Opinion/Essays*, 17 October 1996
[40] Child advocates, Mark Clayton, "To Curb Vancouver's Big Trade in Child Sex, Police Nab 'Johns'," *Christian Science Monitor*, 1997

Souled Out

Children in prostitution are charged 59 times more often than are the male buyers in Vancouver. In six years, only 6 men were charged in Vancouver for buying children in prostitution. Two were convicted. During the same time period, 354 children were charged for involvement in prostitution.[41]

10% of the 100 to 200 women in street prostitution in Calgary, Canada, are under the 18 years of age.[42]

Keep in mind these are the street prostitutes, not the ones that are human trafficked and sold in brothels or in the underground market.

Three men sexually assaulted, threatened to kill and prostituted a 13-year-old girl in Toronto and Oshawa, Canada for 18 months. The men collected $100,000 from selling her as a prostitute. Robert Christian Chattaway, 20, of Scarboro, was charged with kidnapping, aggravated sexual assault, procuring, living on the avails of a prostitute under 18 and having dangerous weapons. Warrants are issued for the two other men.[43]

---

[41] Vancouver: Predator and Pedophile Paradise, a study by John Turvey, executive director of Downtown Eastside Youth Activities Society, Mark Clayton, "To Curb Vancouver's Big Trade in Child Sex, Police Nab 'Johns'," *Christian Science Monitor*, 1997

[42] Helen Dolik "Help group for families is launched" *Calgary Herald*, 11 August 1997

[43] Mike Beauparlant Detective of the Juvenile Task Force, Tom Godfrey, "Child Forced to Hook Man Held After Girl, 13, Assaulted," *Toronto Sun*, 18 April 1998

Jalil Ali-Akbar Bahrami, a violent pimp, convicted of 60 offenses of drug trafficking, assault with a deadly weapon and living off the avails of prostitution was freed from prison and sent to his native Iran after claiming he is not using drugs and that he has found God.[44]

Suspected serial killer Terry Driver, admitted he used prostitutes from the time he was 15, when he gave food to homeless children in exchange for sex. He also admitted that he used three women who were later found dead.[45]

Organized crime by motorcycle gangs, such as 'Hell's Angels,' are involved in drug trafficking and prostitution. More than 50 people have been killed in Quebec over four years, in a turf war between the Hell's Angels and a rival gang called the Rock Machine.[46]

A cocaine epidemic is closely linked with Yellowknife's prostitution and pornography trade. A group of girls were selling sex for cocaine. A man faces trial for trafficking cocaine as well as possessing about 1300 pornographic videos, including some with local

---

[44] Kelly Harris, "Violent Offender Finds God, Is Freed," *Sun Media*, 27 May 1998
[45] Holly Horwood, "Is Terry Driver a Serial Killer?" *The Province*, 17 October 1997
[46] "Canada plans to take on biker gangs," *United Press International*, 23 April 1998

women. Alcohol and drug use was linked to child sexual abuse and trauma.[47]

Many women that are forced into prostitution in brothels in Thailand and many other places are forced to smoke crystal meth to keep them up for days to work hard. They are forcefully addicted to drugs such as heroin and crystal meth in order to keep them working for their drug supply.

Philip Grassi, 49, a Vancouver firefighter and North Vancouver minor hockey coach was arrested and charged for soliciting a prostitute, who was really an undercover police officer. He said his constitutional rights were violated by the Vancouver police department's policy of naming men arrested for prostitution offences.[48]

In my opinion these guys should continue to have their names published to shame them into not purchasing prostitutes. We must do whatever it takes to minimize this trade as much as possible.

Two missing Calgary girls, aged 15 and 16, recruited into prostitution by a sex trade ring on Vancouver's

---

[47] Arlene Hache, Yellowknife Women's Centre, "Coke epidemic in Northwest Territories; Child sexual abuse called root of drug abuse in North," *Canadian Press*, 26 October 1997

[48] Gerry Bellett, "Being Identified As A John Violates My Rights, Says Firefighter: Vancouver father of two takes police department to court," *Vancouver Sun*, 20 June 1997

streets have been rescued and safely returned home. A key factor in solving the case was the use of the Deter and Identify Sex trade Consumers (DISC) computer system, developed by two Vancouver police officers.[49]

Official Response and Action

Police in Sudbury, Canada are launching a *Deter, Identify, Sex Trade, Consumers Program* to combat the growing number of prostitutes, particularly underage girls. The program targets the anonymity of the buyers in order to deter them. Cst. Corinne Fewster, an officer with the Sudbury Regional Police's Drug and Morality Squad said they hope to reduce the demand by targeting buyers.[50]

This is in 1998 and may not have effect since the new laws have passed.

Calgary is one of just two cities in North America where the number of girls in prostitution is declining. Until 1994 when the Street Teams operation began, the number of girls under 18 in prostitution had been rising. There were 400 girls in prostitution or at risk of starting. That figure dropped to 276 in 1996 and 243 in 1997. Every night, Street Teams volunteers patrol the

---

[49] Peter Smith, "Girls Home Safe," *Calgary Sun*, 15 August 1998
[50] Wayne Chamberlain, "Half of Sudbury Prostitutes Under 15 Years Old, Police Say: Streetwalkers a growing problem in Nickel City," *The Sudbury Star*, 13 April 1998

Souled Out

strolls, LRT stations and malls, talking girls off the street and warning those who might be recruited by pimps.[51]

Keep in mind this is 1998, so these numbers may now be higher then they ever were originally.

The British Columbia government pledged $3 million to help street kids and teen prostitutes by hiring more outreach workers and creating "safe houses" in four communities for those who want to leave prostitution.[52]

Canadian Yves Banville traveled throughout Africa (southern Africa, Zambia, and Madagascar) as a sex tourist for months. He collected hundreds of pornographic photos, and raped girls as young as 8. He has been arrested and charged with one count of possession and one count importation of child pornography.[53]

Regulation of the sex industry is being debated by an Edmonton Police Commission task force. The task force is working to keep the sex industry out of residential areas. The establishments of red-light districts and tougher laws will be considered, after information about prostitution has been collected. The Chief of Police

---

[51] Don Braid, "Street Teams Head Deserves Order of Canada," *Calgary Sun*, 15 May 1998

opposes the establishment of red-light districts saying this would contribute to the victimization of women.[54]

NGO Action

Teens involved in prostitution may be helped by a support network that a group in Sudbury is working to create. The group consists of a number of public service groups, community agencies and politicians. Teens enter prostitution for various reasons, including as an escape from an abusive home life, a way to support drug habits, and others are lured into it. Most have low self-esteem, many have been abused in past relationships, and some are parents. A number on Sudbury streets are under the age of 16.[55]

Official Corruption and Collaboration

"If what we're doing is so bad, then why are police officers and politicians some of our better customers?" The range of buyers includes schoolboys to grandfathers, lawyers, top civil servants, businessmen, the laborer *next door*. Most are married. Some are in

---

[55] Debbie Shipley, "Effort under way to reach out to teen prostitutes," *Star*

Souled Out

their 70s. All of their names are on computerized databases in escort agency offices.[56]

From my experience it has even gone as far as priests, judges, police officers and more.

Rural Canadian Mounted Police officer Lyndon Dorrington, 31 was found guilty of soliciting a prostitute after, the woman he approached revealed herself as an undercover police officer. He claimed he was doing research for a course.[57]

Assistant Crown Attorney Agnew Johnston in Thunder Bay, Ontario, was discovered having been exploiting minors for prostitution. He has been appealing disbarment since 1994.

Pornography

Gord Malcolm, former Ajax-Pickering News Advertiser editor, was sentenced to 23 months in jail for possessing and distributing child porn. Malcolm was arrested in a police sting at a motel where he was supposed to meet a 12-year-old girl for sex. 816 images of child pornography and 2,000 images of bestiality and bondage pornography were seized at his residence.[58]

---

[56] One escort agency owner, Nick Pron, "Dating Services Bring Boom Times to Prostitution," *Toronto Star*, 1997
[57] "Cops Research Argument Doesn't Fly," *Calgary Herald*, 8 August 1997
[58] Kevin Hann, "Internet perv behind bars, Ex-editor in kiddie porn sting," *Toronto Sun*, 1 July 1998

Police seized 53 rolls of undeveloped film, three video-cassette recorders, computer equipment, more than 400 videotapes, 15 CD-ROMs and 41 floppy disks from Michael Andrew Gibbon, who is under investigation for offering to sell child pornography on a government Internet website fronting as a pornography site.[59]

Four girls, aged 12-14 were found during a child pornography bust. They were taken into custody by police and released on their own at 4 a.m. The Royal Canadian Mounted Police criticized the Children and Family's Ministries for failure to provide services and protection for the girls.[60]

James Ritchie, a retired military officer who downloaded children pornography from the Internet has been sentenced to 15 months in jail. More than 1,000 images and nearly 700 fictional stories obtained through the Internet were found by Provincial Police. Ritchie was sentenced to 15 months in jail, the harshest sentence since the 1993 Criminal Code amendment targeted child pornography.[61]

Police seized a home computer of a Kitimat, Canada, man containing an album of about 10,000 images and

---

[59] Andy Ivens, *The Province*, 16 December 1997
[60] Stewart Bell & Kim Pemberton, *Vancouver Sun*, February 1998
[61] "Ex-officer jailed for child porn," *Vancouver Sun*, 21 September 1997

Souled Out

video clips of child pornography. Internet cops, from the Coordinated Law Enforcement Unit and Canada Customs, who regularly monitor chat rooms on the World Wide Web, were supplied with the photographs which led to the arrest. The man faces charges of distribution of child pornography and possession of child pornography as a result of illegal activities on the Internet.[62]

Toronto Child Pornography Ring

A police probe uncovered a child pornography business in Don Mills, Toronto, Canada after complaints from the Illinois Attorney General Internet Criminal Activity Unit and Australia. About a dozen girls aged 14 to 16 were filmed naked or with men having sex with them. Digital photos or video of the sessions were transmitted on a child pornography Internet site, which charged subscription fees of $15 to $80. A man had been operating the site for about a year and had about 1,000 subscribers.

 The girls were recruited by the man or a third party and police believe some of the girls were runaways. The man also had access to an agency specializing in child models, which would send him girls. "He would pay them to pose for shots or to have sex," Detective O'Mara said, adding that the cameras were hidden in the apartment. In some instances, the victims didn't know they were being photographed.

I could go on citing examples after examples, cases after cases, but statistics will only raise awareness – not counter-action.

Once again, if you wish to contribute to the battle to
"save the women,"
please don't hesitate to contact me.
www.savethewomen.ca

Souled Out

I am God's Child

*I've been so torn up inside, dazed and confused
Wondered where is my life going, what will I do
I sat there and prayed, day after day
Wondering why did my life ever turn out this way?*

*Then I'd sit there alone and ask myself why
Then I got my answer and I started to cry
It's because I'm God's child and he loves me
He allowed this to happen to set me free!*

*How could I understand others if I didn't feel their pain?
For if I didn't feel it, there would be nothing to gain
To give others empathy, understanding and hope
So I could be there for them while they're trying to cope*

*Life is full of sadness, heartache and pain
We must walk in life humble and not in vain
When we can do this, we can then love ourselves
Finally putting the past upon a shelf*

*What doesn't kill you will make you stronger
For we are not on this earth to be selfish mongers
Our God loves us and he'll give us a spank
When we go down the wrong path, he will be very frank*

*It's because we're his children and he loves us
This is why he allows all the fuss
He loves us and that's why he allows our pain
For he doesn't want his children to walk in vain*

Written by Tania Fiolleau

Tania Fiolleau

CPSIA information can be obtained at www.ICGtesting.com
232076LV00002B/2/P